T0348272

Network-Centred Leadership

How to lead in an increasingly
complex and interconnected world

Charles Carnegie
Dennis McDonald

LONGUEVILLE
BOOKS

First published 2014
for
The Waypoint Group Pty Ltd
by

Longueville Media Pty Ltd
PO Box 205
Haberfield NSW 2045
Australia
www.longmedia.com.au
info@longmedia.com.au
Tel. +61 2 9362 8441

ISBN: 978-1-920681-93-7

National Library of Australia Cataloguing-in-Publication entry

Author: Carnegie, Charles, author.
Title: Network-centred leadership : how to lead in an increasingly complex and
             interconnected world / Charles Carnegie, Dennis McDonald.
ISBN: 9781920681937 (hardback)
Subjects: Leadership.
             Mangement.
             Communication--Computer network resources.
             Technological innovations.
Other Authors/Contributors:
             McDonald, Dennis, author.
Dewey Number: 658.4062

Dedicated to our clients.

Navigating major changes is hard for everyone involved—hard for the leaders taking responsibility and particularly hard for those with little control or visibility deep within organisations. It is a privilege to be included in your journeys.

Contents

Figures, tables and case studies

Figures

Tables

Case studies

Preface

We have written this book for leaders who are operating in a complex environment and managing a diverse portfolio of work. Their work may include managing an organisation, repositioning an enterprise, making a new investment, developing a new strategy or executing a transition.

Our goal is to give leaders a set of indicators, or waypoints, to successfully navigate in complex environments. We do not pretend to provide *the* answer. Every situation is different. Ideally, leaders will combine our approach with their own experience and create a successful way forward for their particular organisations. More generally, the approach should help leaders to apply their own best thinking more regularly and systematically as they seek to deal with increased complexity and information overload.

Our approach is particularly valuable because new social platforms are currently being implemented for enterprise collaboration. These will test and amplify leadership choices. As with any technological transition, some leaders, teams and organisations will adapt successfully and prosper. Many will fail to extract the full benefit.

We have written the book in three parts. Part 1 describes why leaders need a new approach. It focuses on four trends that are disrupting traditional leadership approaches. These are:

- the impact of complexity on strategic alignment and leadership performance

- the importance of collaboration as an antidote to complexity

- the rise of social platforms and collaborative leadership (collectively enterprise collaboration)

- the potential impact of enterprise collaboration on strategy.

Part 2 explains the network-centred leadership approach. It describes the power of networks, discusses leadership and shows how a work-based approach is compatible with common leadership approaches. It then takes these various insights and turns them into a practical approach for dealing with new situations built around four simple questions:

1. Have we clearly **defined** our context?

2. Are we **designing** effective plans and solutions?

3. Have we **developed** capable teams?

4. Are we **delivering** target performance?

Part 3 describes how to execute network-centred leadership. It will help you discuss the four questions with your team and peers in a way that creates an immediate return. You will benefit most if you focus on a specific challenge as you read it.

A simple survey is provided at the end of Part 2 to help you determine how network-centred leadership can specifically help you and your team.

We have written the book in three parts to balance two competing demands: readability and rigour. The result is a book that unfolds in layers. We lay out general ideas, including case studies, in the early chapters to give readers an overall view of our thinking. We then revisit key ideas in the latter chapters and 'unpack' them by providing supporting information and further case studies.

We appreciate that adopting network-centred leadership will have an impact on others; we have therefore aimed to provide a generous amount of supporting material, even if this impacts on the book's narrative. We have also provided a glossary of key terms, notes, references and further reading suggestions at the back of the book.

Who should read this book

Network-Centred Leadership will be most useful for leaders who are already able to:

- **engage in robust discussion**. Turning what are often implicit insights and assumptions into a shared, coherent framework usually requires deep interpersonal engagement and debate between leaders and their teams. If this conversation is to be effective, leaders need to be willing to expose their mental models to scrutiny and discuss them openly. They need to be able to teach and to learn from others.

- **use data and analysis to support judgement**. Network-centred leadership asks leaders to discuss their work, share supporting information and use data as a basis to make and test decisions. Some executives are not used to the level of transparency needed and the different types of relationships (including ceding sole control) that this implies.

- **build capable teams**. Because of the challenges created by greater complexity, leaders will find themselves in situations where they don't know what to do and must rely on others. At these moments, it is important to be surrounded by highly capable teams. This typically only happens if leaders are committed to (a) recruiting and empowering other capable leaders and treating them with respect, and (b) removing people who fail to perform in line with expectations.

- **stand accountable for agreed behaviours, standards and methods**. While network-centred leadership provides great flexibility within teams, it relies on agreed behaviours, standards and methods at the interface between teams. Leaders need to be able to maintain a consistent set of values and behaviours over a period of years. If the quality of these interactions is not enforced, trust is eroded and the system runs down.

- **use information technology**. This is increasingly a prerequisite for effective senior executives. Enterprise collaboration works best when people are comfortable using technology as part of their everyday life.

This book will be published in various forms and edited between printings. We welcome feedback and corrections. Please feel free to email your thoughts and suggestions to us at info@ waypointgroup.com.au.

About the authors

Charles Carnegie and Dennis McDonald are the founders of the Waypoint Group, an Australian consulting firm that focuses on strategy execution and leadership capability development. The ideas presented in *Network-Centred Leadership* emerged from their bespoke work with clients and the insights gained from their online Leadership Effectiveness and Elevation Platform, LEEP.net. To contact the authors, visit www.waypointgroup.com.au.

Charles Carnegie has an honours degree in mechanical engineering from the University of Melbourne and an MBA from Harvard Business School.

Over the past 25 years he has worked both as an executive and a consultant with firms like Accenture, Procter & Gamble, Boral and Cincinnati Bell. At Boral he was a general manager running a series of businesses including asset leasing, manufacturing, contracting and construction. At Cincinnati Bell he helped create the first major ADSL network in the United States in partnership with Cisco.

For the past decade he has been an adviser to boards, CEOs and senior executives on strategy execution and leadership development issues. His experience includes the industrial, technology and services sectors in both the United States and Australia.

Charles also manages the LEEP.net platform and associated research around collaboration and leadership performance.

Dennis McDonald has a first class honours degree in chemical engineering from the University of New South Wales and an MBA from Stanford University. He has more than 35 years' experience in consulting (with McKinsey, Russell Reynolds Associates, McDonald Monahan Associates and Waypoint) to boards and top management in Australia, North America, the United Kingdom, Europe, the Middle East, Africa and Asia on developing and sustaining strategic leadership capability. He has lived in Australia and New Zealand, on the east and west coasts of North America, and in the United Kingdom, France, the Netherlands and Saudi Arabia.

Dennis has assisted the boards of more than 120 companies worldwide in dealing with issues of CEO capability and succession. He has also led a number of management and board audits and reconstructions in top 50 companies in Australia, Europe and North America. Recently, his work has focused on how companies can manage leadership risk by more effectively harnessing internal resources so as to better execute strategies. He works closely with CEOs and their teams in characterising the work associated with the strategy and its implications for their roles.

He is a co-author of *Reprogramming the Board*, a book that focuses on improving the work at the board–management interface.

Acknowledgements

This book would not have been possible without the support of many people.

First, and most importantly, we would like to thank our clients, families and colleagues for all the support, good humour and feedback. It has been a collaborative effort.

We are able to help our clients execute their strategies because we have been fortunate to attend the world's best universities and work in, and with, some of the world's greatest companies. We would like to thank everybody who helped make these experiences possible for us. Both authors have also been deeply influenced by the ideas of Dennis's client and Charles's father, Rod Carnegie.

On a personal note, Charles would like to thank Pip Powell, Elliott Jaques, Jim Wolfensohn, Bails Myer, Helen Nugent, Tony Berg, Martin Koffel and Mike O'Brien for having given him opportunities to learn so much. Finally, and most importantly, he would like to thank Dennis Beausejour for the chance to meet Maile.

Dennis would like to acknowledge the contributions of Andrew Liveris, John Prescott, John Schubert, Ralph Norris, John Grill, David Hoare, Ron McNeilly, Lance Hockeridge, Dick Sibbernsen and Ian Johnson. Without his thoughtful conversations with these leaders over the years, the firm would not exist in its current form.

Over the past five years, we have used Moodle as our own social platform under a General Public License. We want to thank Martin Dougiamas and his team for this foundation. We have tried to recognise all the other people who assisted us along the way via a list of acknowledgements on our website. The latest version, at the time of publishing, is included as an appendix.

As our approach has evolved, we have synthesised various ideas with our business experience and lessons from our clients. We would particularly like to thank Amy Edmondson, Christopher Alexander, Scott Page, Chris Argyris, Tim Berners-Lee, Stephan Haeckel, Michael Mankins, Daniel Kahneman and Amos Tversky, who have provided the foundations for much of our thinking. Our goal is to package and align research from multiple fields to make it useful for our audience of practising leaders. Any valuable insights in this book are inevitably the result of numerous discussions and references. The mistakes are entirely our own.

Finally, this book would not exist without the support of our editor David James and our publisher David Longfield. They have been ably supported by Nick Turner, Anne Healy, Sue Durst and Kiana Weymark.

Introduction

'It is not the critic who counts; not the person who points out
how the leader stumbles, or where the doer of deeds could have
done them better.
The credit belongs to the leader who is actually in the arena,
whose face is marred by dust and sweat and blood; who strives
valiantly; who errs, who comes short again and again, because
there is no effort without error and shortcoming; but who does
actually strive to do the deeds.'[1]
~ Theodore Roosevelt ~

Hundreds of books are published each year on the subject of
leadership. Readers may reasonably ask why we need one more.
The simple answer is that traditional leadership approaches are
failing in an increasingly dynamic and complex environment.
The linear, hierarchical and project-based leadership approaches
taught by companies and universities were designed for more
stable times.

The world has become more complex and competitive over
the past two decades. Regulatory and technical barriers to trade
have fallen. Markets have become increasingly global, intense
and dynamic. Waves of information technology have created new
ways to deliver value and exposed most markets to a broader range
of competitors.

Leaders must now deal with changing goals, evolving strategies,
significant team churn and access to enormous amounts of data.
More stakeholders need to be consulted before a decision can be

taken. Traditional leadership approaches are not designed for this environment.

Leaders at the top of hierarchies cannot process all the relevant information and make all of the required decisions in time, no matter how many back-to-back meetings they have or emails they send. Under pressure, they revert to habitual behaviours and processes that may not be right. What is comfortable, or urgent, often takes precedence over what is important.

For example, we have regularly seen leaders swing wildly between empowerment and control. One senior executive commented:

> We have two seasons in our company. First we focus on customers, empower leaders and preach innovation and flexibility. Then, when something goes wrong, we revert to centralised top-down control. Head office takes over, cuts across our delegations, refocuses our efforts on current markets and defers much of our development activity. We have now got used to the cycle and wait to be told what to do.

When leaders make mistakes, organisations become misaligned, internally and with the market. The wrong problems often finish up being solved, sometimes superbly well. The costs of this misalignment are usually significant for both the organisations and the leaders involved. Companies regularly fail completely. Turnover of CEOs and senior executives is accelerating. On average, strategies only deliver about 70% of their potential.[2]

Enterprise collaboration

Many companies have adopted collaborative leadership techniques to respond to the challenges of a dynamic and complex environment. For example, matrix organisations are common. These started out as organisations with two clear reporting lines across markets and functions but then evolved in various directions. Over time, most large companies have become complex organisations with multiple formal and informal reporting lines and various cross-functional groups and projects.

Now these companies are investing in social platforms. These platforms apply the latest generation of internet technology to enterprises. Examples include mobile tools, intranets, proprietary alternatives to Facebook or Twitter, and online learning campuses. These powerful tools can improve collaboration and break down barriers within, and between, organisations. They allow anybody to broadcast information and connect to a wide range of published information.

The combination of collaborative leadership and social platforms creates a powerful new capability that we call *enterprise collaboration*. When applied successfully it provides new ways for companies to compete and grow.

Unfortunately, it is not always clear how these various collaborative approaches and technologies should be aligned with hierarchy to deliver better business outcomes. Most leaders don't have a way to frame and discuss the changing business context so that the right people collaborate on the right problems, using the appropriate approaches and technology.

People either don't engage, or they engage in ways that fail to create value. Poorly designed collaboration can increase unnecessary consultation and advice seeking, slow down decision making and increase the demands on already busy leaders.

What is needed is a way to explain how the new collaborative tools and approaches fit with hierarchical responsibilities and decision rights so that people know what to do, particularly in changing conditions. Network-centred leadership provides the missing leadership approach.

Network-centred leadership

Network-centred leadership starts by explicitly framing the enterprise as 'work streams'. Some work streams will represent hierarchies delivering stable procedural outcomes. Some will be projects. Some will be complex problems or opportunities that require deep collaboration. Each work stream is represented as a node in a network (called a 'hub' in this book).

Where traditional leadership organises work around roles, network-centred leadership clarifies work and organises people around this network framework. This new approach helps each organisation build a unique picture of the work that needs to be done to create real value. Network-centred leadership also provides a foundation for the effective use of social platforms. Figure 1 provides an example of work streams modelled as a network.

Figure 1. An example of work modelled as a network of hubs

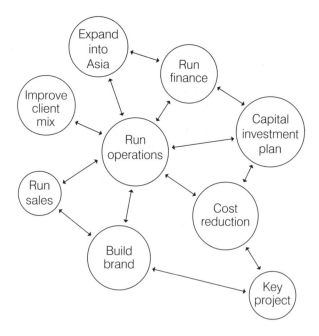

The approach can be applied in stages. As different work streams, leadership approaches and work methods are clarified, the network emerges as a 'map'. This map, and the discussion that accompanies its development, helps to ensure that each work stream and the overall network are explicitly structured and leadership is appropriately distributed.

Over time, the network map captures all the work to run, fix and grow an organisation. It provides a single, shared description of the state of an enterprise at a point in time—its *context*. (In this book, 'context' is an umbrella term that refers to the environment in which a team operates, the team's goals and the choices that it has made. It is described in more detail in Chapter 10.) Learning, knowledge management and innovation can occur within the hubs and across the network.

Network-centred leadership recognises that different work streams require different leadership approaches or methods at any point in time. It provides a common starting point for all kinds of work streams across an organisation. Specifically, leaders at each hub are asked to discuss four questions with their team and peers:

1. Have we clearly **defined** our context?

2. Are we **designing** effective plans and solutions?

3. Have we **developed** capable teams?

4. Are we **delivering** target performance?

Discussing these questions helps to separate what *needs* to be done from leadership structure and roles. Issues can be discussed less personally and with less bias. Just as importantly, regular discussion about the work and its broader context helps to create a shared language and a safe environment for ongoing team communication.

Case Study 1 provides an example of how one organisation created a common context to help it navigate through a complex environment.[3]

Case Study 1
Creating common context in a multinational joint venture

Our client was one of two partners in a joint venture that was designing, and ultimately building, one of the world's largest chemical plants. The scale, complexity and tight timeline placed unprecedented demands on the staff, systems and processes, and external resources. The markets for the plant's products were volatile and subject to significant margin variation, which made it difficult to determine an agreed plant design, let alone a probable range of financial returns.

Each of the partners brought to the project different capabilities and cultures that needed to be accommodated. An organisation was created to deliver the project. It included a steering committee, project management office, front-end engineering design and other directorates. But it was not functioning well when we were engaged.

The key issue was that this new organisation continued to reflect the differing perspectives of the two partners. Simply creating a common entity did not address differences in language, context, priorities and goals.

To be effective, an additional investment in shared context was required. A wide range of leaders from across the world came together to focus on:

- creating an effective leadership team

- aligning the business objectives with the scope of the project deliverables

- identifying and removing 'blockers' that prevented the two partners from working effectively within the joint venture

- building an effective organisation and governance structure

- agreeing on and rolling out the appropriate standard operating procedures.

Collectively, these discussions created a common framework for the joint venture partners and leaders. The project is now close to successful completion, within budgeted time and cost.

Benefits of this approach

Network-centred leadership improves team and organisational performance by providing:

- **clearer communication and context (including goals)**. A network map provides a common language to discuss and manage work that is independent from particular people or roles. It also provides a foundation to align work, capability, information flows and decisions across each team. When change occurs, it gives leaders a shared way to identify the work streams that are impacted by a change, and to communicate with people so they can better understand the impact on their work.

- **better solutions**. When work is considered more objectively, better solutions become possible. Discussion takes the problem out of the mind of the formal leader and allows others to contribute. Teams have the context and freedom to innovate within, and between, hubs in a structured manner. This helps to ensure that the best methods are adopted, rather than the ideas that come most easily to mind.

- **greater alignment and agility between different parts of the organisation and with dynamic markets**. Untangling the various work streams and establishing clear interfaces allows any hub to be changed without affecting the rest of the network. As people become comfortable with the dynamic nature of the network, new collaborative work can quickly be established to fill gaps, using the most appropriate approach and the most relevant leaders. As this process is repeated, the changes to the network can be managed as part of 'business as usual', with less stress to the organisation. Discussion in the heat of the moment can be less personal and less subjective.

- **leadership flexibility**. Leadership can be adjusted on a hub-by-hub basis to meet the changing demands of the work at hand. Companies can continue using hierarchical and project-based methods when they are effective. They can use more flexible collaborative approaches to address emergent problems. And they can switch between different approaches to optimise performance when circumstances change. This is because the approach treats leadership as a design variable that is regularly adjusted to meet the changing needs of the work. Leaders can be assigned to work in a less biased way. There can also be greater regard for the effects of cognitive overload.

- **greater capacity to manage complexity**. Dealing with complexity used to be the exclusive domain of CEOs and a few leaders at the top of organisations. These people could frame reality with reasonable clarity and create a reasonably stable environment for the rest of the organisation. But as markets become more dynamic, this is no longer possible. A much broader group of leaders are now exposed to complexity and they need to be engaged in the conversation so that they can perform and represent the organisation appropriately. A network framework allows this broader group to work together effectively.

- **a framework to support the use of social platforms**. The power of social platforms is increasing exponentially. As with previous generations of information technology, there will be winners and losers. The particular patterns of collaboration that are being 'hardwired' within, and between, organisations are likely to create new sources of advantage. Success will depend on the level of alignment between the strategy of the firm, the structure and culture of the organisation, and the technological choices being made.

  A network map exposes the web of leaders and relationships that create value across the organisation. Social platforms can then be aligned with this leadership architecture to support valuable collaboration. As things change, leaders can update their part of the map and provide everybody with a shared picture of what is happening—as it is happening. Everybody can confirm the current state of their work streams and their position in the evolving broader network. This allows information to be shared and issues managed without relying on a few individuals, endless meetings, or emails.

Part 1

Why leaders need a new approach

Chapter 1
Leadership challenges in a complex environment

'In the old economy, the challenge for management was to make product. Now the challenge for management is to make sense.'
~ John Seely Brown ~

The increasingly dynamic forces shaping the commercial environment are making the job of leaders much harder. While traditional hierarchical and project-based leadership approaches continue to work relatively well in stable and predictable situations, they are increasingly breaking down in complex environments.

This chapter explains how and why these breakdowns are happening. Failure is rarely the result of incompetence or ill will. Poor performance usually occurs because leaders are overloaded and organisations have become misaligned.

Leaders today face a more dynamic environment

Forty years ago, industry structures were stable and markets followed relatively predictable cycles. Management was mostly a linear process, involving discrete steps supported by established management disciplines. Circumstances have changed. Deregulation occurred in many countries and markets, barriers to competition have broken down, and the world has become much more dynamic and unpredictable.

Today, leaders face an environment that is both more complex and more complicated. It has been well described by others as a 'VUCA' environment (volatile, uncertain, complex and ambiguous).[4] Various forces have become significantly more dynamic over the past 20 to 30 years; for example:

- **Commercial and political uncertainty has increased as historical barriers to trade have fallen**. Reduced trade barriers have created a more volatile and interdependent global market. Political risk is becoming a major factor in developed economies as minority agendas can rapidly gather momentum. Deregulated financial markets and global money flows have created new sources of volatility.

- **The volume of information has increased**. By minimising the cost of creating and transmitting content, the internet (including social platforms) has allowed a new level of connectivity within, and between, companies. Leaders are now made aware of many more issues and details, both internally and externally. Both the number of information sources and the amount of information have increased. Moreover, a multitude of new filters and considerations are available, making information management profoundly more complicated than it was a few decades ago.

- **Public scrutiny has become ubiquitous**. New communication methods, and the 24/7 news cycle, have led to an ongoing public discussion about companies, programs and people, much of which is outside the control of anybody involved. It is now virtually impossible to stay abreast of all the relevant news, let alone shape it.

- **New business models have changed the nature of competition**. A range of new business models have revolutionised entire industries, allowing individuals to start and scale up businesses that can quickly compete with even the largest organisations. In 1958, a company that made it into the S&P 500 index could expect to stay on the list for 61 years. Today the average is just 18 years.[5]

- **The workforce has become more mobile and diverse**. People now move between countries, industries and companies with increased frequency. The result is that teams are typically made up of people who have worked together for less time, and have less in common, than ever before. These teams can bring more ideas and experiences to creative problem solving. However, they typically have fewer shared experiences, use different languages, work in different locations and have more diverse goals for their careers, making alignment challenging.

These changes create both opportunities and risks. Volatile markets, changing political environments, new technologies and new business approaches are inherently unpredictable. The impact on each team and enterprise will be highly sensitive to small differences in the leadership of each organisation.

We call these kinds of environments *complex* environments. They can only be defined by reference to the various dynamic forces that shape them on an ongoing basis. Figure 2 shows how this book represents a complex work environment.

Figure 2. A complex work environment shaped by dynamic forces

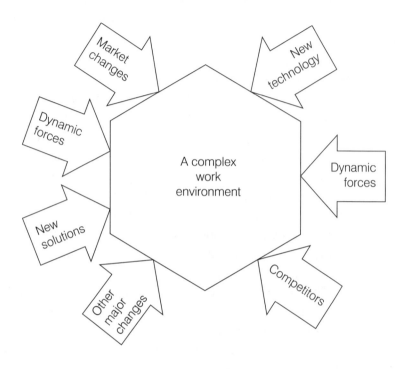

Dynamic forces create misalignment

If leaders are to capture opportunities in volatile markets, they first need to understand the impact that dynamic forces are having on leaders and organisations. This understanding starts by considering exactly what leadership is.

All leadership is concerned with organising people to work in an effective manner in order to deliver valuable outcomes. The challenge is that different people may want to do different things, use different methods or target different outcomes. Well-known leadership approaches, like hierarchy and project management, resolve these differences by assigning a leader who controls key decisions. The leader sets direction and the rest of the team follow. The success or failure of any leader or approach depends on how well they align teams, methods and goals to produce valuable outcomes. Success can be represented as a Venn diagram (Figure 3).

Figure 3. Alignment of goals, methods and outcomes through successful leadership

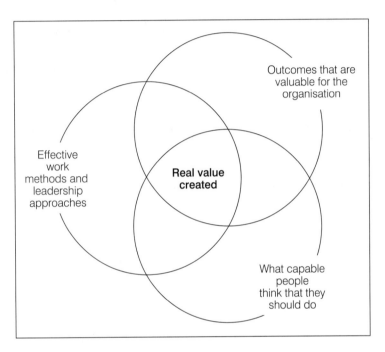

Dynamic forces and complexity make it harder for leaders to align the three elements shown in Figure 3 to create real value. All three are pulled apart from each other:

1. What is valuable for an organisation becomes less clear, because markets evolve and customer priorities change. Leaders and teams need to learn to hit a moving target.

2. Leaders are less likely to know what to do, or be able to provide clarity for teams. The uncertain relationship

between cause and effect means that a leader cannot be sure of what methods to use, or how actions will be interpreted.

3. When traditional approaches break down, people may decide what to do independently. They may revert to embedded behaviours—for example, 'follow orders', or 'listen to the customer'. These are not usually a good proxy for what really needs to be done. People also start to question whether what is being proposed is consistent with their own best interests. Nobody wants to be associated with failure.

The tendency for methods, people and outcomes to become misaligned is shown in Figure 4.

Figure 4. Misalignment in complex environments

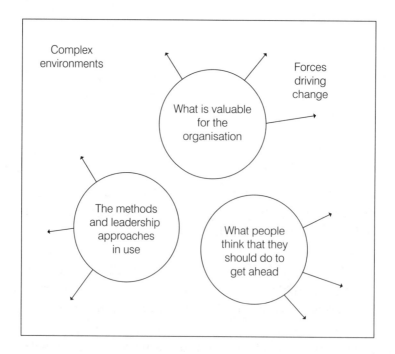

Addressing the various sources of misalignment puts increasing pressure on the few leaders who are at the top of the project or hierarchy. Change introduces confusion. Targets shift. Eventually, a point of inflection is reached when the pace of environmental and organisational change exceeds the knowledge and processing power of the leader in charge. At these moments, traditional leadership approaches break down and momentum is lost.

One small example of this phenomenon occurred when a CEO and executive team decided to change the annual budget process from a bottom-up activity—taking several months and led by the finance function—to a top-down exercise driven by the operational leaders. The process was successfully completed and signed off by the board in only three weeks. However, two months later, one of the operational leaders found his entire finance team were still working on the bottom-up exercise. When he asked why, he was told, 'Because our key performance indicators (set by the central finance function) require it and they haven't been changed!'

Leaders commonly respond by restructuring

Often, leaders address misalignment and underperformance by restructuring. Typically, they replace and reshuffle people, and realign reporting relationships.

Such initiatives can help to create alignment across organisations and fill gaps in communication between, and within, business units. Structures such as matrix organisations can be highly effective and improve the capacity to better manage resources against multiple dynamic objectives.[6] They are a sensible response to the need to be coordinated across multiple dimensions: markets, products and functions.

However, restructuring typically creates a number of additional sources of complexity for leaders:

- **Any change process can be disruptive**. Objectives and communication can be unclear. Employees need to work through a range of issues and questions to be comfortable. Time and effort are consumed internally.

- **Roles can become less clearly defined**. Leaders reporting to two or more hierarchies may have difficulty building alignment, or allocating resources to the various business lines, functions and local geographies.[7] Managing internal relationships to ensure alignment can become a job in itself.

- **Organisational churn can become the norm**. In some cases, leaders are being forced to continually refine their strategies, realign accountabilities and redirect resources quarterly, if not monthly, as they seek to meet changing customer requirements in the global market. Project teams are quickly brought together to deal with an issue and then disbanded. Structural changes, as a result of realigned accountabilities, have reduced 'in role' tenure for many senior executives. Often, they last less than two budget cycles. Organisational memory is consequently becoming less reliable.

- **The work of senior leaders typically becomes broader and more dynamic**. The work of the senior leadership team has changed from what was a relatively predictable annual planning cycle, with clear accountabilities, to a collaborative, real-time, iterative process where agility, speed of decision making and continuity of context become critical success factors. Being the sole individual with the 'right' answer is rarely possible any more. Supporting the right person to do the right work, within the right context and at the right time, has become progressively more difficult and important.

All this change creates a demanding environment for leaders

The combination of dynamic external forces and ongoing internal change creates a demanding management environment for leaders. For example, Waypoint has worked with a global resources company for more than a decade. Over that time, the company has had to learn how to manage in an environment of increasing complexity. Sources of variability included:

- **the volatility of commodity and financial markets**. The company traded daily in a number of dynamic markets, both as a buyer of raw materials and as a seller of finished products. It also faced volatility in the financial markets. Both kinds of volatility were exacerbated by the global financial crisis of 2007–2008, which caused demand to plunge and lowered prices for our client's commodity products. The company also faced financial pressure due to the collapse of the capital markets.

- **the surfacing of market-driven opportunities**. The company made two acquisitions and several minor divestments, and initiated a large joint venture project in the Middle East.

- **changing internal expectations**. When the CEO sought to lift the company's performance to a new, sustainable level, the behaviour of his management team, helped by some new additions, began to change. He adjusted both his leadership approach and organisational structure to match his transformation strategy.

Regardless of the cause, the leaders throughout the organisation found that they needed to adapt continually. The challenge was to create internal and market alignment on a continuous basis. The leader had to adopt a strategy that matched the volatile market conditions. He had to adapt his internal structure to accommodate the acquisitions, and develop ways to capture the best aspects of the culture within these acquisitions. And he had to find ways to meet his more ambitious targets. All this required thinking about the right network and creating a seamless alignment between consumers, staff and investors' expectations.

Understanding the new environment

The new environment consists of both more and different kinds of work for leaders. The most challenging is dealing with complexity, where goals become fluid and new methods and solutions need to be invented. Examples include the creation of new revenue streams, deal making, capital investments, market shifts of various kinds, technical research and development, innovation, and changing, or unclear, governance arrangements.

In these situations, nobody knows the 'right' way to think about the problem and there is no reliable process to follow. Smart people must come together and find a path forward, usually through trial and error. Most leaders have not been taught to recognise these kinds of problems, much less resolve them.

The matrix in Figure 5 can help leaders and teams to discuss and assess the state of a particular environment and identify complexity. The environment is classified according to two dimensions: the clarity and alignment of the goals that are being pursued, and the clarity of the relationship between approach and outcomes. Leaders cannot control the environment that they encounter, but if they use the matrix, they can better clarify the situation and respond accordingly.

Figure 5. Types of work environments

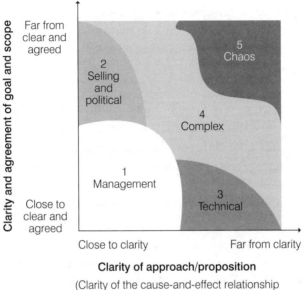

Clarity of approach/proposition

(Clarity of the cause-and-effect relationship
between management actions and outcomes)

Note: Adapted from the Stacey matrix.

The matrix identifies five kinds of work environment that a team may encounter:

- management environments, which have clear goals and a clear and agreed relationship between cause and effect

- selling and political environments, which require persuasion and the building of coalitions to address differences in goals

- technical environments, which require deep analytical ability and expertise in the subject matter to properly manage causes and effects

- complex environments, which have patterns that, if correctly framed, can be recognised and acted upon—they are dynamic, however, and require ongoing analysis

- chaotic environments, where there are no patterns of any kind.

For simplicity, the book talks about two different work environments: traditional environments (1, 2 and 3 in the matrix) and complex environments (4 and 5 in the matrix). Enterprises typically have some of each type of work environment across their organisation.

Leaders are used to traditional environments and work in them successfully using well-established hierarchical and project approaches. Even when one dimension of the work is unclear, traditional management approaches continue to be effective if appropriate capabilities are added to the team.

That is not the case in complex or chaotic environments. In these complex environments:

1. **goals are neither clear nor agreed**. Sales executives and politicians are accustomed to this kind of environment, but it is a new experience for many managers.

2. **the relationship between actions and outcomes may not be clear**. In complex environments, small changes in initial conditions, or direction, can produce significantly different outcomes. Marketers and researchers are used to proposing and testing hypotheses, but this can be an uncomfortable process for leaders who are accustomed to being in control.

To remain effective in complex environments, leaders need to move from solving known problems with established methods to the creation of new solutions and methods in real time.[8] This requires more collaborative methods that focus on learning and experimentation.

Dynamic environments create cognitive overload

For most organisations, at least some part of their environment has become complex. To be successful, senior leaders and teams need to use different approaches for each different kind of work. They need to transition seamlessly between the efficient problem-solving techniques that work well in traditional environments and the design-oriented approaches that are needed to create tomorrow's solutions.

This is hard. Leaders tend to be caught by three forces:

1. They are overloaded by the volume of information they must process, the diversity of stakeholders they must manage, and the breadth of issues they must confront.

2. Mental models that leaders have relied on to process this information are increasingly unreliable in a complex environment.[9] Goals keep changing and assumptions about cause and effect often prove wrong.

3. A number of cultural and human biases encourage them to ignore the risks presented by the complexity of the new environment. Rather than getting help, they carry on as usual, relying on their intuition.

Many leaders, teams and organisations reach a point of inflection where the pace of environmental and organisational change leads to confusion. Shifting targets mean that leaders find it difficult to establish a point of departure, let alone get a clear idea of where they want to finish up, or how they want to get there.

Without an appropriate framework, they reach a condition described as cognitive overload.[10] In this state, they don't have a way to understand and integrate the different kinds of work that they now need to do. They lack the mental models to process the various goals, filter the right information, prioritise the most important business needs and communicate appropriately.[11] They may also be unable or unwilling to access suitable support.

When leaders are in cognitive overload they tend to make some of the following errors:

1. **Receiving or selecting the wrong inputs**. Humans prefer information that fits with what they know, or which reinforces their domain of expertise and feelings of self-worth.

2. **Using intuition to solve problems when they should be using reasoning**. Reasons for this error include oversimplification, misclassification of a problem (to make it fit with prior knowledge) and/or avoidance of the problem to limit personal exposure.

3. **Applying an inappropriate historical mental model to a new situation**. Even historically successful approaches may not produce the same performance if they are not properly adapted to the new environment. Without this adaption, leaders may solve the 'wrong' problem. Overconfidence bias may also cause leaders to overestimate the success that historical approaches will have in the new environment. Research shows, perversely, that the less you understand a situation, the more confident you are likely to be. As the philosopher Bertrand Russell said, 'The trouble with the world is that the stupid are cocksure and the intelligent are full of doubt'.

4. **Prioritising work based on personal capability or preference as opposed to business need**. Simply put, people do the work that they are comfortable with, instead of the work that most needs to be done.

5. **Reacting emotionally or inappropriately to a new situation or problem**. There are a range of reasons why this may occur, including fear and greed and a range of other inappropriate behaviours.[12]

Figure 6 provides a model of how executives think.

Figure 6. How executives think

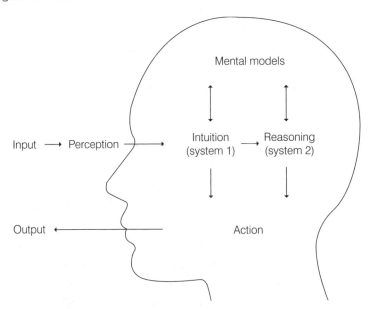

Note: This diagram is our representation of the work of Kahneman (2011).

Executives use two different mental systems to make decisions. Inputs from various senses arrive at the brain via the perception centres (eyes, ears, etc.). These are then processed by either intuition or reasoning. In both cases, leaders rely on mental models, either consciously or subconsciously, as a reference. The key elements are as follows:

- **Intuition** is fast, parallel, automatic, effortless, associative and emotional. It is the unconscious part of your brain that does most of the thinking, most of the time—for example, how people respond when they meet others is typically an intuitive response.

- **Reasoning** is slow, serial, controlled, effortful, rule governed, flexible and neutral. People are conscious of this kind of thinking and may find it difficult or 'clunky'. Learning a new language or a detailed problem analysis are examples of this kind of thinking.

- **Mental models** are conceptual representations of the past, present and future that can be evoked by language. These may include programmed responses to social cues, frameworks and processes. The various diagrams in this book are examples of these kinds of models.

The cost of leadership errors is significant

The consequences of cognitive overload and misalignment are not very appealing. For a program leader, there is about a 70% rate of failure.[13] Complex organisations seem to generate a 'gravitational pull' that drags leaders into focusing too much on the tactical detail of their roles. Even apparently capable leaders can get bogged down in reactive 'firefighting'. In these conditions, leaders fail to capture the value implicit in their strategy and competitive position. This, in turn, produces a range of highly negative consequences for the leader, the organisation and investors.

At the extreme, companies fail and leaders are terminated. On average almost 30%[14] of the potential value of a new strategy is lost due to failures of leadership. The same types of leadership failures repeatedly occur (Table 1).

Table 1. Percentage of total strategy value lost by type of leadership failure

Type of leadership failure	% of total strategy value lost
Poorly communicated strategy	5.2
Actions required to execute not clearly explained	4.5
Unclear accountabilities for execution	4.1
Organisational silos and a culture of blocking execution	3.7
Inadequate performance monitoring	3.0
Inadequate consequences or rewards for failure or success	3.0
Poor senior leadership	2.6
Uncommitted leadership	1.9
Unapproved strategy	0.7
Inadequate skills and capabilities and other obstacles	0.7
Total average loss of value due to leadership failure	29.4

The likelihood that a particular organisation or program will lack the right kinds of leadership to address these failures is called its leadership risk. This risk commonly appears as a steady drag of wasted activity (disagreements between divisions, miscommunication, delay and rework that reduce momentum and enthusiasm on a day-to-day basis). It can also lead to major failures and missed opportunities, particularly in periods of crisis.

Case Study 2 provides an example of leadership failure in the face of complexity.

Case Study 2
An example of leadership failure

A CEO had built a strong reputation as an individual who could successfully complete large, complex projects and deliver outstanding results. A group of investors sought him out to run a listed start-up company that had acquired the global rights to build and operate a rare metals refinery and associated mine in Australia, utilising existing port and associated infrastructure. The share price rose steadily as the project took shape. Communications with the market were frequent and transparent, as the company sought to set financing in place. A highly qualified European firm was carrying out front-end engineering and design.

Then complexity struck! Unforeseen environmental and operating issues arose, leading to a change in direction. A decision was made to move the project to a country in the Middle East where there were adequate supplies of the required mineralisation, cheaper sources of power and government incentives for exporters, including a tax-free zone and low-cost trained workers.

While these changes addressed some of the issues, they also introduced several new sources of complexity. The CEO had never operated overseas, let alone in a country where English was not the native language. Port facilities had to be constructed. Government regulations had to be navigated. The financiers were not happy with the increased political risk.

The CEO found that it was a daunting task to deal with a board in Sydney, a project team spread between Europe, the Middle East and Australia, and front-end engineering and design contractors in Europe. Signs of leadership risk started to emerge almost immediately. The start date for construction was delayed. Costs rose further, putting pressure on funding. The delays caused rifts in the relationship with the Middle Eastern partner.

The CEO refused to change his leadership approach. He would not accept that he needed help or that the project was in trouble. He insisted that he could deliver 'his way'. Finally, his team began to 'abandon ship' and the shares plummeted from more than $4 to a fraction of a cent. The project was abandoned, the rest of the team was fired and only a company shell remains.

Today's environment means that leaders will face shifts in strategy more commonly. To avoid the fate of the CEO in this case study, leaders need to be aware of changes in their work, recognise gaps in their own capabilities and redesign their leadership approach and teams as appropriate.

The opportunity is equally significant

It is easy to view dynamic markets as a threat to traditional business models and careers. They are. However, they can also be viewed positively. Dynamic markets create opportunities for innovation, new solutions and revenue growth. Leaders and organisations that can learn to manage effectively in a dynamic environment and capture these opportunities will materially outperform those who can't.

While success will obviously require talented leaders with the requisite character, skills and experience, it also matters how leaders work together across an organisation. Complexity can overcome the capacity of any individual, no matter how talented. The performance of the organisation depends on how effectively the broader group of leaders across the organisation work together.

Organisations with the right leadership frameworks are thriving. Their leaders can work together effectively and avoid cognitive overload. Case Study 3 illustrates how one leader was able to provide an appropriate framework to help leaders manage after the global financial crisis of 2007–2008. It helped to turn 12 independent and 'siloed' country leaders into a powerful region-wide cohort whose performance set the standard for the rest of the company.

Case Study 3
Turning independent country leaders into a high-performing cohort

Our client restructured their organisation's global business portfolio to create a regional structure led by three regional leaders and a number of country managers within each region. The leader of the European, Middle East and Africa (EMEA) region asked us to help clarify the new approach with his team. At this point he was dealing with the impact of the global financial crisis of 2007–2008.

Within the EMEA region there was a cohort of 12 country managers. Some operated in mature markets with major manufacturing sites within their country borders, serving the wider EMEA market. Others were operating in relatively immature markets with significant growth potential. They all faced different commercial challenges and needed different limits of authority.

English was a second language for all the country leaders. Our task was to help create a common business language that everybody understood, and which identified the work that needed to be done within each country. It was necessary to facilitate conversation among the country managers, and between the business and functional leaders.

Developing a shared understanding of context, and an appreciation of each other's programs, was critical to accelerate the development and execution of local market initiatives and to ensure that, where appropriate, an aligned approach could be taken across country and industry borders.

We created a hub on our Leadership Effectiveness and Elevation Platform for the EMEA country managers and the regional functional leaders. The team used the hub to summarise the transition that the corporation was undergoing and explain the 'from/to' behaviours and the work of each manager. We helped develop country charters (Figure 7) and work templates that would serve as a guide. Managers began thinking through how they would drive the change program and extract maximum value from their respective markets.

Over time, a network map emerged. Each manager's output was discussed and could be challenged by the other country managers and the regional functional leaders. This approach allowed everybody to see who was collaborating, and adjustments were made accordingly.

Figure 7. Clarifying work using a country charter

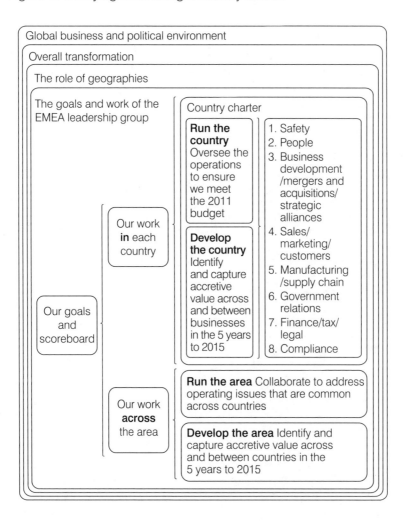

We then worked with individual country managers to help them articulate country priorities and develop an implementation timetable. These programs, which were executed collectively, formed the basis of the work of the EMEA region for at least the subsequent 12 months.

The outcome of this investment was that common procedural issues were handled efficiently, leaving time to focus on the specific challenges in each country. Country managers had a language to discuss their issues with each other and find new solutions. The EMEA region outperformed all of the other regions during and after the global financial crisis, despite the turmoil in individual country economies.

Chapter 2
Collaborative leadership can provide a solution

'In individuals, madness is rare; but in crowds, it is the rule.'
~ Friedrich Nietzsche ~

The challenges of complexity, overload and misalignment are not new. Companies and academics have trialled and reviewed a myriad of organisational forms and technologies to align people in dynamic environments. The solution is properly structured collaboration—an essential element of network-centred leadership. If executed well, collaboration can provide an answer to the challenges of information overload, poor decision making, program underperformance and leadership failure. However, it is hard to execute for a variety of reasons.

A definition of collaborative leadership

The term 'collaborative leadership' is used to convey a wide range of ideas. To avoid confusion, this book uses the term to describe ways that teams can work together effectively in complex environments. In this context, collaborative leadership is an iterative and incremental approach to create solutions in a highly flexible and interactive manner. Trials and pilots are used to test assumptions and aid learning. Phased delivery is used to ensure that each investment of resources produces real benefits. This kind of approach has been deployed broadly in information technology, problem management and new product development projects (it includes techniques like design thinking, teaming, Scrum and Agile). A more detailed description is provided in Chapter 8.

Collaboration is not optional in complex environments because solutions require a range of strategies and knowledge that are beyond the scope of any one person's abilities. In these cases, no single leader knows all the relevant areas of business, or the cause-and-effect relationship between work and desired goals. An iterative, collaborative approach is the only viable way forward.

Specifically, collaboration helps leaders and teams to:

1. **capture the best thinking from everybody in the room**. So long as people have relevant expertise and can be aligned, this produces demonstrably better outcomes.

2. **encourage teams to spend some time searching for appropriate models, frameworks and solutions that they might want to use.**[15] When this is not done, leaders may use the management approaches that most easily come to mind, rather than the ones that best fit the current context.[16]

3. **encourage a specific discussion about the forces shaping the environment and the assumptions that are being made about key parameters**.

4. **ensure that the agreed approach for achieving goals is available to all**. Team members have a point of reference, so they can contribute more independently. They don't always have to include the leader when issues arise.

5. **provide a point of departure when the environment inevitably changes**. Solutions can evolve to suit changing conditions.

Companies are investing in collaboration

Companies understand the value of collaboration and are investing in it heavily. There is little choice. The complexity of the environment has exceeded the processing capacity of many organisations. The key limits are:

1. **Conventional matrixes can't accommodate the number of dimensions that require coordination**. Matrixes were initially designed to provide coordination across two well-described, and relatively stable, dimensions. Now, thinking that there are only two dimensions seems quaint. Leaders are required to coordinate activities across multiple dimensions, including products, markets, geographies, functions and capabilities.[17] This is beyond the capability of a formal matrix structure because a single person can only sensibly report to a few individuals.

2. **The annual planning process is no longer sufficient**. Leaders face the same challenges integrating strategy, technology and organisations that they have always faced. However, the increased pace of change means that this work has become an ongoing iterative process for many leaders. Different approaches need to be managed in parallel. With the increasing rate of change, hierarchical and project-oriented approaches can become redundant before the planning process has been completed.

3. **The mix of work that needs to be performed has changed as a result of changing industry structures**. Collaborative leadership was developed to provide leadership across functional and organisational boundaries. As organisations become more connected into global supply chains and markets, this kind of leadership is becoming increasingly important.

4. **Technology is increasing the potential for decentralisation and open communication**. For better or worse, technology is increasing everybody's access to information and ability to communicate. Controlling access is increasingly difficult.

Companies are also investing in social platforms

Social platforms are the next generation of internet technologies.[18] Platforms include Google Docs, Salesforce.com and various offerings from Microsoft. These are a powerful new set of tools that allow people to use phones, tablets and computers to capture information, organise it coherently and then distribute the new knowledge to other people. Platforms such as Facebook, Twitter and LinkedIn have shown how users can interact and collaborate with each other as creators of user-generated content in a virtual community.

The goal of these new platforms is to formalise and empower horizontal leadership approaches that can help to deliver results across divisional, functional and organisational boundaries.[19] This is not a new idea. The 'water cooler' or 'grapevine' has been a well-established feature of organisations for decades.

The combined application of leadership and technology[20] elevates and empowers this informal network to the point where it is increasingly the primary method by which work is achieved in an organisation. When these platforms are being implemented to formally facilitate collaboration across the organisation, the approach is called enterprise collaboration.

Enterprise collaboration represents a profound opportunity

When enterprise collaboration is well structured and aligned to strategy, it can dramatically increase the processing power of an organisation and free leaders from cognitive overload. It encourages transparency, provides equal access to information, breaks down hierarchical structures and provides support for unfiltered communication and feedback.

The last management change that was remotely similar was the quality movement. In the 1980s, management thinkers encouraged the control and continuous improvement of processes as an alternative to hierarchy[21]—Japanese automobile industry companies made investments to explicitly manage their production organisations through a range of quality and cultural initiatives. Others did not. They avoided the issues, or hoped for the best. The consequences of failing to make this investment were profound for the industry worldwide. They are still being felt in Detroit today.

Enterprise collaboration using social platforms has the potential to deliver a similar level of competitive advantage. Just as the quality movement dramatically impacted 'blue collar' productivity, this next shift can have a similar impact on 'white collar' productivity.[22]

Enterprise collaboration introduces two significant risks

The benefits of collaboration have been well understood for decades but the approach has not been broadly adopted. The personal and organisational investments required to create a collaborative environment are usually only made when a compelling business imperative arises and management is forced to adopt the approach.

The major problem is that collaboration is neither easy, nor risk free. Real collaboration is a deeply social process that is susceptible to a whole range of human reactions, biases and prejudices.[23] It exposes gaps in a leader's knowledge, allows team members to question assumptions, and crystallises disagreements about methods. This creates challenges at two levels: the corporate and the personal.

Corporate implications of enterprise collaboration

To better understand how enterprise collaboration affects leadership, it is worth reviewing the development of leadership over the past 30 years. In the 1980s, hierarchical leadership was the most common leadership approach. It was supported by an annual planning and budget process. Back then, the 'big idea' was reducing the number of layers of management to a sensible level.

Since that time, the range of leadership approaches has widened, in part because of the availability of new communication and information systems. In crude terms:

- The 1990s focused on project leadership supported by personal computers and email.

- The 2000s saw the rise of matrix organisations and the internet.

- The 2010s are poised to see the rise of collaborative leadership and the use of social platforms.

Each decade provides another set of options. The development of these leadership options is shown in Figure 8.

Figure 8. Development of leadership approaches over the past 30 years

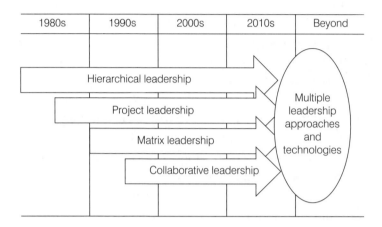

Now, many organisations are managed using a combination of four approaches:

1. an annual change management process that includes strategy, budgets and performance management

2. a hierarchical organisation of some kind—this may be a matrix of two or more dimensions

3. formal project teams focused on specific goals

4. a collaborative social network of some kind supported by email, calls and other communication devices. This is increasingly being facilitated by the organisation to some degree, via social platforms.

These four approaches were historically used in a clear priority order. The strategy and shape of an organisation were confirmed once a year by the annual planning round. Leaders in hierarchical organisations managed the organisation to execute these plans and control variation. Projects were established and the informal networks filled in any gaps.

However, when collaboration is enhanced by social platforms, the traditional order gives way. The four approaches start to be used in parallel and given equal standing in an organisation. Different problems get worked through different channels, using different methods and technologies.

Organisations are evolving to reflect these overlapping leadership approaches. They still use a hierarchical or matrix skeleton, but they also formally use a wide range of cross-functional projects and social platforms to establish direction, exert a degree of control and navigate increasingly complex environments. We call them *complex organisations*.

The risk is that people are not clear about how the various requests and instructions that they receive should be prioritised. People working below the senior team are not sure if they should be working to the annual budget, the project the CEO launched mid-year to address a customer concern, or the request for assistance from a peer. If this confusion is not addressed, there is little chance a leader will be effective.

Personal implications of enterprise collaboration

Collaboration also challenges leaders at a personal level. To collaborate effectively, leaders need to be willing and able to describe and discuss assumptions and complex problems. This can be hard. And it can be frightening—both for the leader and the team. Concerns range from looking stupid through to loss of employment. People simply will not participate in a collaborative process if they don't understand and accept the personal risks.

More generally, people like to believe that a leader or organisation can provide clarity and certainty about direction, work and employment. These beliefs are challenged during periods of significant change. There is understandable anxiety which can discourage collaboration.

Thinking in traditional environments

In traditional environments, leaders frequently have deep expertise about products and markets and are well prepared to make forecasts. They typically make plans and allocate people based on this expertise. People can then simply do their job as part of the leader's overall design.

Implicitly, these leaders are using a set of assumptions about how the world works that may be subconscious and intuitive. As plans are executed, lessons are learned and approaches refined. This is called 'single-loop learning'. The key elements of the approach are shown in Figure 9.

Figure 9. Single-loop learning as part of a traditional leadership approach

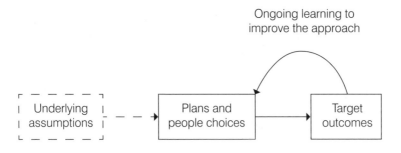

As described in Chapter 1, assumptions about organisational structure and business operations are increasingly being broken down. For managers, the value that has traditionally flowed because they 'know' things is evaporating in a world of social platforms. Just as the *Encyclopaedia Britannica* has been challenged by the free Wikipedia, leaders no longer have a significant information advantage over others.

How people think when they are collaborating

When real collaboration is in progress, a process called 'double-loop learning' occurs. In this kind of learning, a second loop of discussion is created to make assumptions explicit. They are then challenged and refined by the leader and the team. Progress occurs not only because the plans are being improved by the discussion, but also because the teams have a clearer understanding of the problems they are trying to solve and the range of methods available to deal with them. This process is represented in Figure 10.

Figure 10. Double-loop learning as part of a collaborative leadership approach

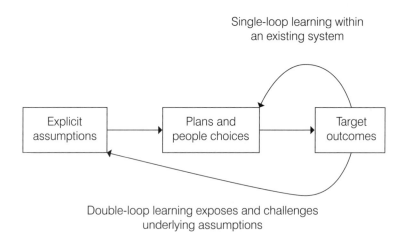

Single-loop learning within an existing system

Explicit assumptions → Plans and people choices → Target outcomes

Double-loop learning exposes and challenges underlying assumptions

Collaboration introduces a range of risks into any planning process. Executives have often invested a large part of their careers and identities in specific methods, tools, positions or beliefs. Collaborative planning conversations can expose and challenge these positions and assumptions by creating options that make particular methods, tools and positions redundant.[24]

Not surprisingly, disagreement is common. Making changes can make positions and specialist knowledge redundant. Everybody wants the 'others' to buy into their framework—not change their own behaviour to suit other people.

Defensive reasoning

When challenged, individuals can consciously or unconsciously adopt 'defensive reasoning' to protect their position and underlying assumptions from review (Figure 11). A range of defensive behaviours may emerge. Individuals can:

1. **disengage**. That is, they simply withdraw from the conversation. Justification includes being busy, thinking that the conversation is unnecessary, or other devices. In many cases, they revert to embedded traditional leadership behaviours.

2. **display a range of defensive behaviours**. They may become angry, inconsistent, incongruent, competitive, controlling, fearful of being vulnerable, or manipulative.

3. **create defensive, ineffective group relationships**. These include splitting teams into parts where nobody has all the information to be successful without the leader and the use of 'power politics'.

4. **adopt a defensive mindset**. This may include mistrust, a lack of risk taking, conforming to process, emphasising diplomacy, concentrating on power-centred competition, and rivalry.

5. **collaborate around safer but less important issues**. Not all collaboration is of equal value.

Figure 11. Defensive reasoning

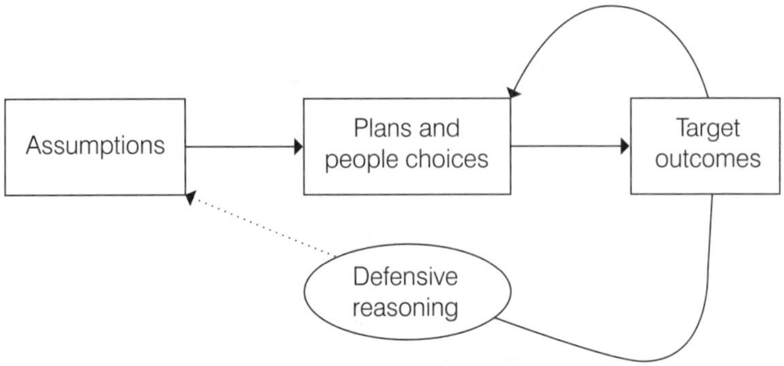

Defensive reasoning hinders a proper review of
individual assumptions

Effective enterprise collaboration

Some companies are better than others at managing the risks associated with enterprise collaboration. When researchers study effective collaboration, they find that three quite different things are required to make it work successfully: psychological safety, a clear framework for decision making and leadership, and leaders with the requisite capabilities.

If leaders and organisations are to gain real value from their collaborative investments, they need to understand and provide each of the three factors required for effective collaboration.

Psychological safety

The key social factor required for healthy collaboration is psychological safety.[25] This refers to the ability of each team member to make a contribution without incurring negative consequences. It does not imply a careless sense of permissiveness, or an unrelenting positive reaction in the hope of creating cohesion. Rather, it is creating a sense of confidence that the team will not embarrass, reject or punish someone for speaking up. For example, before asking a question, seeking feedback, reporting a mistake or proposing an idea, individuals might ask themselves, 'If I do X here, will I be hurt, embarrassed or criticised?' If the answer is 'no', the environment is psychologically safe and collaboration will proceed.[26]

Psychological safety is a much more specific idea than trust. It relates to the behaviours of a group of people in a particular team, over a particular period of time, in relation to a defined piece of work. Trust implies that the leader will look after the individual, despite changing circumstances. While people would obviously like the kind of assurance that trust implies, it is usually beyond the power of the leader to deliver it. By contrast, psychological safety is a reasonable, necessary and achievable goal.

The Chatham House Rule provides an example of how psychological safety can be created.[27] It is different from the more general concept of trust. The rule states:

> When a meeting, or part thereof, is held under the Chatham House Rule, participants are free to use the information received, but neither the identity, nor the affiliation of the speaker(s), nor that of any other participant, may be revealed.

This agreement gives individuals (usually diplomats) the opportunity to speak freely at a meeting, but does not make any promise of trust between the participants.

There are at least seven sets of issues that impede the creation of a psychologically safe environment for collaboration. Where appropriate, they need to be recognised and managed. The risks are:

1. **lack of agreed rules for team behaviour**. If a leader and team are unable to agree on and enforce a set of basic disciplines, collaboration probably won't work.

2. **specific career risks**. Periods of change contain significant risks for leaders and teams. Most obvious is the risk of loss of employment or advancement. These concerns are both real and significant. Even if the threat isn't real, the threat response and defensive behaviour can be a problem in itself.

3. **personal agendas**. Everybody in an organisation is legitimately pursuing a personal agenda relating to compensation, job security, advancement or recognition. People have a lot to gain and lose when there are major changes in the direction of a team or organisation. If these agendas are not well managed, they can undermine team goals.

4. **increased language and preference diversity**. Under pressure, people want things to work their way and be described in terms that make sense to them, regardless of the implications for others. This can reduce commitment to shared goals, common language and shared experience across most groups.

5. **legal risk**. Legal concerns can reduce the potential for real feedback and communication, imposing an ethic of 'political correctness'. The unintended consequence of this can be the curtailment of a team's ability to speak frankly and build real trust.

6. **increased number and range of stakeholder demands**. Transparency has increased the number of people who feel they should be consulted on a particular issue. An example of this problem is that meetings cease being task focused and are instead expanded to become information forums.

7. **increased access to management literature**. The ease of access to management literature now means that research

is available to support most positions, no matter how ludicrous.[28] When people don't like an idea, they can usually find 'research' to defend their position, making alignment more difficult.

A clear framework for decision making and leadership

Leaders and teams need a framework that explains when and how collaboration and social platforms are being used. The new technology and organisation need to be aligned with the strategy and the formal hierarchy. Leaders cannot assume that people will know how to process the various messages racing around an organisation.

Unless a framework is provided, it is hard to see how collaborative activity, including the use of social platforms, can produce meaningful outcomes. Social media has exploded because it helps individuals pursue their own interests and collaborate in new ways. Some leaders believe that the same thing will happen in organisations. Enormous value will be created by the 'wisdom of crowds'. History (and the quote from Friedrich Nietzsche at the start of this chapter) reminds us that there is considerable evidence to the contrary.

The challenge is that in an enterprise environment, collaboration is a means to an end, not an end in itself. To be effective, collaboration needs to be used in combination with other leadership approaches to produce valuable outputs.

We regularly see leaders commit to an overly distributed leadership architecture when things are going well, only to revert to a 'command and control' approach at the first sign of trouble. Company-wide investments in leadership development, design thinking and innovation are replaced overnight by cost reduction.

We recommend breaking the organisation into parts so that appropriate innovation, leadership and collaboration risks can be taken. Initially this is hard work, but it creates manageable groups with specific goals where psychological safety can be established and real value created.

Leaders with the requisite capabilities

Senior executives are not naturally humble. Most are highly motivated, even driven. Otherwise they would not be where they are. When hierarchies are the dominant organisational structure, self-awareness is not paramount. The structure allows leaders to exert power within the enterprise in order to create a collective intent that matches the needs of the market.

Projects can have similar dynamics. The project leader is authorised to control the overall integration of the activities through the setting of goals and timelines. Although they have less direct control over people and activities, leaders still enjoy superior decision rights and a broader set of information about the overall project.

In complex environments, when collaboration is required, these key strengths can become weaknesses. Different capabilities are required because no-one, including the leader, is likely to have a full picture of what is going on. A suitable response can only be achieved collectively. This requires leaders with collaborative capabilities. For example, Laszlo Bock, the senior vice president of people operations for Google, values executives who can learn, share power, take ownership when required and show the humility to step back and embrace better ideas from others.[29]

Chapter 3
Social platforms amplify collaboration

'The existing structures and processes that together form an organization's operating system need an additional element to address the challenges produced by mounting complexity and rapid change. The solution is a second operating system, devoted to the design and implementation of strategy that uses an agile, network-like structure and a very different set of processes.'[30]
~ John Kotter ~

Social platforms have been used for enterprise collaboration for about a decade. In that time, a wide range of trials and corresponding developments have emerged. A second round of enterprise collaboration platforms are being launched and are likely to be widely adopted. Organisations are still experimenting to determine how best to use the technology because best practice methodologies are not yet clear.[31]

Despite the uncertainty, social platforms have now been adopted widely enough to suggest that they will become mainstream in the coming years.[32] Older managers will have seen a range of similar transitions over the past few decades: personal computers, email, the internet. In each case, a point was reached when adoption of the technology became inevitable. Anybody who wanted to stay employed was forced to adapt, even if it was not clear to them what to do with the new tools.

Looking forward, any discussion about collaboration will inevitably include a discussion about supporting social platforms because their value is increasing rapidly. For better or worse, the next generation of employees uses social platforms as their first choice to work, communicate and entertain themselves. Organisations that cannot provide and use these tools are unlikely to be able to attract and retain the best talent from this generation of 'digital natives'.

This chapter provides a high-level overview of social platforms. Even leaders who don't want to use social platforms should understand them. They are being adopted by customers, suppliers and many employees and are already shaping critical markets, such as recruitment and services more broadly.

Types of social platforms

Currently, business communications remain centred around the individuals in a team, or hierarchy. People are separated in time and space and communicate via a series of individual interactions. An individual publishes a report, sends an email, or makes a call or a decision; different people have access to different information and then use different approaches to make decisions. To create shared understanding or to take a shared decision, people have to physically come together in a meeting.

When social platforms are established, anybody can be connected with anybody else. Commands, instructions and requests can zoom across the globe in an instant. Everybody can be part of every piece of work of the executive agenda.

Social platforms store all the information centrally and automatically create a record of all the process steps that occurred in a discussion or decision. Everybody is continuously connected to the evolving work through computers, phones and tablets. This change in communication patterns is shown in Figure 12. When leaders know what they are trying to achieve and teams are aligned, social platforms are likely to accelerate performance and deliver significant benefits.

Figure 12. Social platforms change communication flows

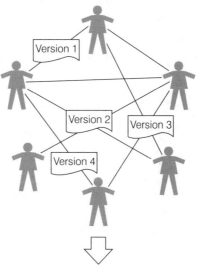

Current communication patterns

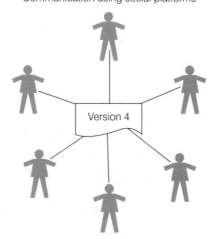

Communication using social platforms

To get a sense of the potential of the new technology, we will briefly consider four examples of social platforms: social networking, cloud-based applications and searchable storage, content management systems, and online campuses. Each of these represents a new way to communicate, collaborate and manage knowledge. Each has the potential to improve or disrupt leadership work and productivity.

Social networking

The functionality driving Facebook will inevitably become part of the communication suites of most organisations, along with video chat, instant messaging and other applications. Like email and phone calls, these are useful communication tools and are quickly being adopted. Once installed, any pair of employees can start using social tools without regard to the rest of the organisation.

Cloud-based applications and searchable storage

The organisation can collaborate more directly once applications for managing documents move from individual personal computers to the cloud. Two common examples of this kind of platform are Microsoft 360 and Google Docs. Whereas before individuals worked on different versions of documents, they can now work centrally. This is much more than just version control. People genuinely collaborate on work at the same time, supported by video and voice communication, without the need to be in the same room.

This has obvious benefits for productivity, control and speed.[33] Individuals and small groups can elect to adopt the platform one document at a time, creating a new searchable content resource for the organisation.

Content management systems

In content management systems, broader teams work together to collect, manage, process, share and then distribute information throughout an organisation. These systems create so-called 'information factories' that can be used, for example, to develop and manage key processes and projects. Typically, a content management system such as Microsoft SharePoint or Google Docs is used to underpin an information factory.

The consequences of adopting a content management system can be profound. In the traditional environment, work was 'owned' by an individual at any point in time. People could say different things and provide different information to different people because everybody maintained an individual perspective. With a content management system, everyone on a team is literally on the same page.

This increase in transparency has a number of implications. The team has to agree to a single description of the program of work and stay aligned to this agreed language and approach. While it is still possible to keep information private, this is no longer the default.

Online campuses and learning management systems

Social platforms can also be used for learning. Online learning has been developing at a rapid pace over the past decade. Educators have thought deeply about the creation and sharing of mental models that are coherent, valid, persuasive and adaptable. They spend their lives leading cohorts of students to higher levels of thinking and new behaviours using online platforms.

Technically, learning management is the capacity to design content and activities that achieve learning outcomes for a cohort. Whereas content management is a process for managing information socially, learning management is a way to engage people and change the way they think and behave.

For complex issues, when the work is challenging and the team is variable, online campuses are particularly helpful.[34] Small differences in the quality of knowledge transfer can produce meaningful differences in enterprise performance.

Benefits of social platforms

Used well, social platforms have real utility and, in many cases, adoption is likely to be successful. Proponents claim that social platforms will improve economic performance by:

- improving the quality of both content consumption and collaboration[35]

- effectively bringing diverse expertise and knowledge to bear on strategic and operational priorities

- accelerating organisational learning and knowledge management

- addressing the challenges of information overload

- improving decision making.

A number of companies and organisations have adopted flatter, more flexible organisations and achieved the kinds of benefits listed above. The most profound examples of this approach are the open-source communities that produce and support open-source software and content. These include Linux, Apache, Mozilla, Wikipedia and Khan Academy.

Implementation challenges

While social platforms can deliver substantial benefits to an enterprise, the technology alone does not necessarily improve the performance of leaders or organisations. To date, social platforms have been applied in approximately 70% of major companies but most of them have derived only a limited benefit.[36]

Many of the issues associated with effective collaboration were discussed in the previous chapter. Implementation of a social platform tends to raise many of the same issues from a technical perspective. In order to achieve the full value of the technology, each implementation needs:

- **alignment of goals, language and experience.**[37] Social platforms can provide new methods for the creation, distribution and consumption of content. However, like email, quantity is no guarantee of quality.

  Think of the disconnect that happens between sales and delivery in many organisations. Each group pursues different goals. They produce information in different formats, for different audiences. They also discuss issues in different ways, with different vocabularies. All of these issues come into play when the two groups are connected by a social platform.

  If leaders and teams have not clarified their goals, approach and communication, formal project management and mass communication resources can turn small areas of uncertainty into organisational confusion. People can become confused and may go off in their own direction, exacerbating the leader's problems of strategy execution.

  In one instance, a company proposed to change its business model. The CEO, who had imagined this change for a couple of years, assumed that everyone understood why a change was necessary and what would be different in the new organisation. An external group was engaged to communicate the realignment using pictures. The senior team individually described the change and its benefits. The resulting diagrams were an amalgam of these views but they failed to emphasise the key elements that the CEO had tried to communicate to his team. This created a misleading view of the business opportunities and priorities for many people. These small misunderstandings multiplied across geographies, businesses and functions, leading to significant concern and confusion. The issues were eventually addressed, but momentum was lost due to the creation of unnecessary leadership risk.

- **leaders who are willing and able to participate in enterprise collaboration**. Social platforms can amplify the challenges associated with collaboration. They eliminate personal boundaries and give everybody a bigger voice, inside and outside the team and organisation. To be successful, leaders need the skills to navigate the radical transparency, equality and connectivity that social platforms provide and engage directly in the collaborative process.

- **a level of social trust among the users**. Collaboration relies on social trust, supporting incentive and ingrained habits. If these are not in place across an organisation, implementing a social platform is unlikely to be successful. In these circumstances, activity is likely to focus on information that is politically safe and of low value,[38] and not especially important to organisational goals.[39] In competitive cultures, social platforms are likely to be used to pursue individual, not organisational, goals.

- **social conventions for advice seeking**. Social platforms encourage people to ask for more advice before making a decision. They reduce the costs and barriers so people can seek advice from a wider range of people.[40] This can provide significant benefits for the advice seeker if they ask the right people. The advice seeker can then integrate the diverse responses to create better decisions and innovative solutions.

Advice-seeking behaviour has a downside, however. The algorithms in social platforms recommend approaching the highest profile individuals across the whole company, which concentrates most of the advice seeking on approximately 5 to 15% of the population.[41] The impact of this on the productivity of those highly valuable people is often negative.

In addition, this new culture may undermine self-reliance and impede decision making. If everybody is encouraged to consult and get input for every decision, things slow down and key people get overloaded.

- **information filters**. Leaders need common and appropriate filters to process the many streams of information that social platforms generate. Either people will not know what to do with the new tools, or they will lose essential focus on their own work as they seek to stay abreast of the work of others. While this may be interesting to an individual, it may not be relevant to the outcomes that they have to deliver. This disconnected activity may expose leaders or encourage people to go off in their own direction.

  To get the benefits of the technology, social platforms need to be integrated into the day-to-day work processes of the team and organisation.[42] Work processes, data structures and organisational forms need to be consistent in both the real and online world. This inevitably means undertaking a very specific analysis to align the various hierarchical and social processes that will be used to run the organisation.

- **an adaptable technical platform**. 'Rapid change' and 'software' are not words that usually go together easily. It is self-evident that platforms need to be set up so that they can be changed over time. What is often overlooked is that the platforms have to support the adaption of the large datasets that they contain. Shared folders are extremely flexible but the data in them can become disconnected and less valuable over time, especially if structures become less relevant.

- **various dimensions of security**. Beyond the obvious need for technical security in any platform, there lies a broader range of issues. The goal of social platforms is to promote the sharing of valuable information. This goal has to be balanced against the risks of oversharing, which may result in the loss of intellectual property, breaches of confidentiality or loss of reputation.

Unless these issues are addressed, there is a very real risk that social platforms will be little more than another source of confusion and frustration in the lives of leaders, who are already struggling with cognitive overload.[43]

Fortunately, some social platforms provide a range of data that describe the level of engagement and learning that is taking place. These measures can be used to diagnose and correct issues in real time.

Successful application is likely to require some experimentation

The benefits of social platforms and the associated implementation challenges are difficult to predict. Our experience internally and with clients is that implementing these platforms requires a combination of technology, content, use case and leadership. This typically requires an iterative development effort. Case Study 4 describes the journey we have taken to learn how best to use social platforms in our own work.

Case Study 4
Enterprise collaboration using a social platform

Since 2009, Waypoint has been developing and using a range of social platforms. We started with content sharing using SharePoint. As we began to better understand the differences between content transfer and knowledge transfer, we switched to create an online campus based on Moodle, an open-source learning platform used by more than a million teachers and 30 million students worldwide. We have developed this into our Leadership Effectiveness and Elevation Platform (LEEP.net).

The creation and development of LEEP has been an iterative process. When we started we didn't appreciate how different social applications could be. We have now implemented almost 50 hubs to support a wide range of collaboration, learning and knowledge management projects. In total, we have trained several hundred leaders and created a large number of content folios. A model of the LEEP network is shown in Figure 13.

No two implementations have been the same. Differences occur because using a social platform for knowledge work challenges people to work in a new and more transparent way. Each team will respond differently based on their unique combination of:

- business use case, i.e. the value proposition for the use of the platform.

- technical installation

- user experience including documentation

- content

- leadership

- user behavioural change.

Clarifying and integrating the various elements of each successful implementation takes ongoing work, discussion and attention over a period of years. Teams need to learn and improve their approach, technology and documentation on an ongoing basis.

For example, as we have implemented LEEP at Waypoint we have been challenged to:

- make our corporate processes and assumptions clear for everybody in the team

- document and distribute a common language via a glossary

- observe the real-world behaviour of hundreds of leaders over extended periods of time and adjust our thinking accordingly

- sort all the firm's information into a single structured curriculum

- tag and describe each piece of information so people know its purpose

- configure and manage their own groups. This requires decisions about users, permissions, content, structure, functionality, etc.

- measure the engagement and capability of users

- provide tailored feedback and ensure that our communications are persuasive

- develop work materials collaboratively. In practice, this means that most members of a team are both creating and consuming content on a daily basis, learning and teaching as they go.

When teams are willing to do this work, the results are significant. When it is not possible to develop enough momentum to establish the platform, the team typically returns to traditional methods with a greater understanding of the issues.

Figure 13. Waypoint as a network of social platform hubs

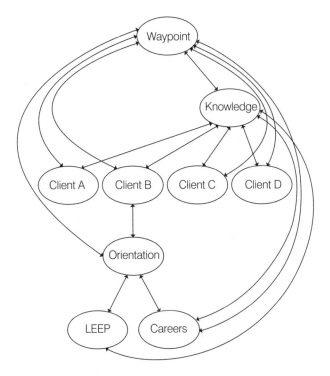

Chapter 4
Enterprise collaboration—
the winners and losers

'Several technological and political forces have converged, and that has produced a global, Web-enabled playing field that allows for multiple forms of collaboration without regard to geography or distance.'
~ Thomas Friedman ~

Some leaders are already using enterprise collaboration to successfully navigate complex environments. They are reorganising to make the best use of the new technologies and capture benefits at both the revenue and cost lines. It is clear that these initiatives will have a significant impact on companies and industries over time.

We expect clear winners and losers will emerge. Leaders who have a coherent framework to align their strategy, technology and organisation will find new ways to compete successfully, despite complexity. They will use enterprise collaboration to:

- quickly and effectively transfer digital capabilities and knowledge globally

- leverage the productivity of knowledge workers

- develop the relevant skills and capabilities of leaders and organisations.

Trends are starting to emerge that explain how enterprise collaboration can provide a valuable basis for competition more generally. This chapter describes these trends and identifies the factors that will separate successful leaders from the rest.

Information technology trends are well established

Over the past 20 years, waves of information technology (IT)—computers, software, mobile phones, networks and the World Wide Web—have been broadly adopted. Collectively, they have been a major force driving market dynamics, organisational change and increased competitive intensity.

Four trends have emerged from this digital competition:[44]

- **facilitation of global competition**. Global trade has grown materially in the past two decades, supported significantly by improvements in IT.

- **less discrete industry structures**. Only about 40% of a company's profitability can be explained by industry structure.[45] Increasingly, different companies in the same industry are producing different levels of performance.

- **more 'winner takes all' markets**. Industries are consolidating, with an increasing amount of market share going to a few companies.

- **greater turbulence**. Companies rise and fall more rapidly.

Companies within an industry respond to each wave of technology in different ways. Each company will build a unique combination of strategy, organisational form and technology to deliver its products and services. Different companies will generate very different levels of performance, depending on how well they use the new technologies. Start-ups or international competitors will use new technology to enter the market. These differences accumulate over time, so companies enjoy very different futures, despite starting in the same industry. Then the cycle repeats—winners misapply a generation of technology and lose their competitive position.[46]

Organisations that used to compete with companies of broadly the same size and shape are increasingly finding themselves facing competition from different sources. New entrants appear in markets at a lower scale than in previous eras. Businesses grow more easily and to a larger scale than was formerly possible using traditional approaches. The speed with which a generation of internet start-ups has grown provides an example of these trends.

IT platforms allow new digital capabilities to be created and distributed

As industry structures have broken down, strategists have moved to think of enterprises in terms of core capabilities. Companies compete by owning and organising core capabilities into a variety of useful products and services.[47] Leaders can reapply these capabilities as markets evolve.

Capabilities may represent physical things like business units,[48] plants, offices, data centres and call centres, as well as digital capabilities like brands, maps, datasets, processes and designs. These different kinds of capabilities have very different characteristics.

People are familiar with the impact that the internet has had on digital products, such as music. More broadly, IT allows companies to make and distribute a range of digital products, processes and knowledge in a similar way. Improvements to an operating model can be embedded into software and then distributed across a company or industry.

Digital capabilities are powerful because they are created through innovation, not capital, and the scale can be increased at a low marginal cost. To demonstrate, consider two retail chains that are in competition. Both have equally good ideas to improve store performance: one by improving a process, the other by upgrading a piece of equipment. The first can upgrade the logistics system and train the people to distribute the improvement to all their stores, all very effectively. The second needs both capital and time to upgrade the equipment at every store.

Companies are increasingly competing globally, which also means that they are competing on the basis of their digital capabilities. When the difference in valuable knowledge exceeds the shipping costs associated with physical capabilities, markets can change rapidly. Costco Wholesale Corporation, for example, which operates an international chain of membership warehouses for retailers, can successfully enter Australia, despite the Australian market being the world's most concentrated retail environment. The reason: Costco's digital capabilities, such as store design, business model and pricing strategy, are clear and strong.

Enterprise collaboration will extend these trends to knowledge work

Most of the previous waves of technology have optimised operational processes. The number of people in process roles has now shrunk as a result of streamlining, outsourcing and automation.

More than 40% of all employees are now knowledge workers of some kind and are required to use judgement in their roles.[49] It seems likely that enterprise collaboration will mainly be used to help the performance of these knowledge workers. This segment of employees is large, growing and expensive. It represents a significant opportunity to improve corporate productivity and performance.

Estimates suggest that enterprise collaboration may yield productivity improvements of 20 to 25%.[50] Improvements are likely to come in a variety of ways, including:

- improving productivity in both quality and cost terms, which may occur by automating or eliminating low-value work or by better allocating work between knowledge and process workers

- complementing knowledge workers with supporting technology, allowing them to innovate and create new sources of knowledge

- better combining groups to create new knowledge and capabilities—this collaboration can form the basis for innovative new products and services

- better transferring knowledge across leaders working on similar problems in different industries or geographies

- supporting better leadership, innovation and knowledge management approaches.

There is unlikely to be one 'right' approach

To illustrate how social platforms might be applied, consider two of the United States' most successful business leaders: Andy Grove of Intel and A. G. Lafley of Procter & Gamble. Each is widely respected and profoundly successful. Yet they approach leadership in very different ways.

Lafley was the chairman and CEO of Procter & Gamble as it rolled out its portfolio of established brands across every market worldwide. He thought hard about the work of the CEO and wrote about the four things that only a CEO can do:[51]

1. defining and interpreting the meaningful outside

2. deciding what business you're in

3. shaping values and standards

4. balancing present and future.

This approach created clear alignment. It allowed him to bring in innovation from outside, either through partnerships or via acquisition, and then to distribute products globally with great efficiency.

By contrast, Grove never thought that only one person was leading Intel. To him, there was always a shared power structure. He encouraged people to test new techniques, products, sales channels and customers. He delegated authority deep into the organisation using simple rules like 'allocate our limited wafer capacity to the most profitable products'. Grove stated:

> A corporation is a living organism; it has to continue to shed its skin. Methods have to change. Focus has to change. Values have to change. The sum total of those changes is transformation.[52]

For its first 15 years, Intel was in the business of designing and making memory chips. It had engineers to design both new chips and production processes, and production plants that turned silicon wafers into valuable chips. By the 1980s, however, the memory business faced increased competition. Intel needed to transition from making memory technology to making microprocessors. Interestingly, by the time the senior team had faced up to the need to change, the transformation was already well underway within the company. The 'maximise wafer profitability' rule had already led the production and planning departments to move most of the capacity from memory chips to processors.

Each approach to leadership has value. Lafley's focus on four kinds of leadership work produced clarity and alignment. Grove's willingness to delegate created flexibility and innovation. One can speculate that these two leaders would make very different social platform choices. Consider, for example, the balance between empowerment (encouraging people to make decisions themselves) and alignment (teaching people to make decisions in an agreed way).

Social platforms can support either approach. The four examples of social platforms described in Chapter 3 can be roughly arranged on a spectrum between empowering individuals at one end, and having tight organisational or team alignment at the other (Figure 14).

Figure 14. Focus of various social platforms

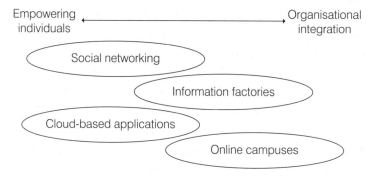

At one end of the spectrum, the introduction of social networking seems to have moved the balance of power dramatically towards the individual. It tends to remove information inequalities.

- **Inside the organisation**, it becomes easier to do things either yourself or in small groups. Environmental and organisation churn means that broader investments in training and relationship building are often wasted.

- **Outside the organisation**, it is much easier for individuals to band together and capture the economies of scale that used to be restricted to organisations. In a complex evolving market, small groups can create sophisticated new solutions and scale incredibly quickly.

When employees are highly motivated and self-directed, the results are invariably strong. However, if they are not, it leads to the question, 'How are you going to get a return from all these people when they are off doing their own thing?'

In the middle of the spectrum are cloud-based applications and information factories, which provide new tools to support various kinds of work such as document collaboration, process management and strategy execution. Each, in its own way, lets organisations align authority and responsibility. They empower the people who have the best information and skills to make decisions in a timely manner.

At the other end of the spectrum, online campuses have dramatically improved corporate learning and compliance by giving all employees access to training on a continuous basis.

The right platform for any organisation will depend on a range of factors, but once it is installed it is hard to change. When correctly matched to a strategy and organisation, a social platform will enhance performance. Conversely, a lack of alignment will undermine the enterprise's competitive position.

Strategies will vary based on the kind of business

Enterprises can be divided into three types based on their primary value proposition: operational excellence, product leadership, and customer intimacy.[53] In each case, a different combination of strategy, knowledge management, leadership and technology is required to create valuable digital capabilities.

Social platforms as a driver of operational excellence

Operationally excellent businesses deliver a combination of quality, price and ease of purchase that no-one else in the market can match. They operate streamlined processes that minimise cost and provide hassle-free service. They are standardised, simplified, tightly controlled and centrally planned, leaving few decisions to rank-and-file employees. Examples of this type of business model include Costco (wholesale warehouses), Southwest Airlines (transport) and McDonald's (fast-food restaurants).[54]

Social platforms can benefit these businesses in a variety of ways. They can reduce information technology costs by providing cloud-based solutions, improve the quality of demand forecasting, provide better visibility and control over operations and input costs, improve training and development, and improve the quality and cost of service delivery. But social platforms can also introduce risks. The individual empowerment associated with social networking may distract leaders and reduce their focus on cost and service.

Social platforms as a driver of product leadership

Organisations pursuing product leadership continually push their products into the realm of the unknown, the untried or the highly desirable in order to expand their performance boundaries. A product leader's proposition to customers is to provide the best product or service—period. Examples of this type of business model include FedEx (parcel delivery), Intel (electronics) and Johnson & Johnson (medical and pharmaceutical goods).

These businesses focus on the core processes of invention, product development and market exploitation. They usually have a flexible business structure and systems that reward new product success and do not punish the experimentation that is needed to get there. They have a culture that encourages individual imagination, accomplishment and 'out of the box' thinking.[55]

Social platforms enable a range of tools to help these companies improve creativity and productivity. For example, 'big data' analysis (the analysis of large and complex datasets) will identify many new relationships that will spark ideas and suggest new ways forward. Crowdsourcing—turning to online communities for ideas, content and services—will bring diverse skills sets to problems at very low cost. The platforms will support knowledge transfer and learning across the organisation, changing the dynamics of innovation and creativity.[56]

One key factor that will differentiate competitors is how social platforms will be used to affect the relationship between creativity and organisational size. On the one hand, the technology allows individuals to group together and to achieve the benefits of scale by being in a community without being in a formal organisation. On the other, it reduces barriers to innovation and collaboration 'inside the firewall'. The best innovation will depend on how particular networks form.

Social platforms as a driver of customer intimacy

Customer-intimate organisations are able to build deep relationships with individual customers or niche markets. They compete based on a superior understanding of the customer and how to deliver 'the right total solution for you'. Businesses with this value proposition have an obsession with the core processes of solution development (helping the customer to understand what is needed), results management (ensuring that the solution gets implemented properly) and relationship management. These businesses delegate decision making to employees who are close to the customer. They have a culture that focuses on deep and lasting client relationships. Examples of this type of business model include Nordstrom (department stores), Four Seasons (hotels) and Boston Consulting Group (consulting).[57]

Social platforms will help these firms by supporting their efforts to create deeper customer relationships. A broad range of information sources should help these kinds of organisations to better understand the issues facing their customers. Market research and customer profiling will allow more tailored offers. Community engagement platforms will help create deeper relationships.

The potential to improve service and to lock in relationships with social platforms is compelling. However, it is a double-edged sword. A stronger customer relationship for one firm inevitably means a loss of market share for somebody else.

Summary of the current leadership environment

A few key factors shape today's leadership environment.

- The market environment has become more complex and dynamic. Traditional leadership approaches break down in these environments because they demand too much from the few leaders at the top. The pressure leads to cognitive overload in leaders and growing misalignment within, and between, organisations. The result is significant underperformance by leaders, teams and organisations.

- Enterprise collaboration is seen as the solution. This involves creating an additional horizontal communication network within, and between, companies supported by the use of social platforms. This second network can address alignment issues by working freely between, around and through the established structure.

- The combination of enterprise collaboration and traditional leadership approaches has created complex organisations. Multiple leadership approaches are being used in parallel.

If organisations are going to be successful, they need to provide their leaders and teams with a coherent framework to collaborate and make decisions that are compatible with the organisation's strategy and hierarchy. This new framework needs to increase flexibility without a loss of control, an increase in cognitive overload, or greater misalignment—otherwise the new social platforms will simply undermine the traditional approaches and create confusion. Leaders and companies that fail to create an appropriate framework should expect to underperform compared to those who do.

A successful collaboration framework will:

- align the various reporting lines, information flows and decision rights

- help create an environment of psychological safety where people can contribute without fear, which is a very different challenge to the installation of a software platform

- provide a basis for the development and management of digital and leadership capabilities that can provide a competitive advantage in complex environments.

These challenges will be hard for many leaders, who may need to adjust their leadership approach and upgrade their skills to adapt to the new environment. This is not a transition from one approach to another; it requires a more agile and flexible approach that can accommodate both traditional approaches and collaborative solution development.

More broadly, social platforms are likely to produce winners and losers. The performance of these platforms is progressing exponentially. Some enterprises will be able to develop new digital capabilities and compete effectively in new markets. Others will simply create confusion for leaders and their teams, and exacerbate the problem of cognitive overload.

Part 2

A description of network-centred leadership

Chapter 5
Leaders need to be more explicit about their work

'If I had an hour to save the world, I would spend 59 minutes defining the problem and one minute finding solutions.'
~ Albert Einstein ~

All leaders are managing a portfolio of work of one kind or another. These portfolios may range from navigating political relationships to establishing operations or solving new problems that emerge in the market. For the sake of simplicity, let's call each of these relationships, issues, problems and activities a *work stream*. In one way or another, every leader is prioritising and executing a list of some kind.

Network-centred leadership provides a new way to clarify and manage this list using a network framework.[58] The approach takes all the goals, opportunities, problems, tasks, systems and risks (collectively the work streams) and puts them into context using a network map. This map provides everybody with a shared point of reference and a common set of information on a continuous basis.

Used well, a network can:

- accommodate both complex and traditional environments

- align collaborative and hierarchical leadership approaches

- clarify interfaces and interrelationships

- filter information flows

- balance flexibility with control

- facilitate the delegation of non-critical decisions.

In summary, a network-centred approach helps to ensure that the right people are working on the right things using the appropriate tools, despite change.

What do leaders have to do?

Any leader in an organisation can start using network-centred leadership. It is a steady, incremental approach that complements matrix organisations. It is not a radical change that requires the support of the CEO to implement.

To get started, the leader and team should pick a piece of work and discuss four questions:

1. Have we clearly **defined** our context?

2. Are we **designing** effective plans and solutions?

3. Have we **developed** capable teams?

4. Are we **delivering** target performance?

These four questions are effective across a wide range of environments from a strict hierarchy to decentralised chaos. They give everybody a common starting point to discuss the situation and develop a way forward. Leaders can work through the four questions with their team when circumstances change or whenever they encounter a new issue.

If leaders and teams talk through these questions collaboratively and record the answers consistently, they will build a shared understanding of the context in which the team or organisation operates. They can then prioritise the problems that need to be addressed, decide on the methods to be used and build the capabilities that are required.

Most of the time, a leader will quickly check off the questions, update a relevant document or two, and move on to execution. At worst, they will spend a little time confirming what everybody already knows.

Sometimes, the discussion will expose assumptions, identify questions or locate gaps, which can reduce risk. Team members will have a way to ask clarifying questions in a safe manner.

Finally, there are situations when leaders know none of the answers to the four questions, and they need to start from scratch. Here, network-centred leadership provides a consistent way to work through the challenge or opportunity.

Leaders who work through this structured process are forced to stop and think. They can deliberately filter their inputs, reason systematically, expose their mental models and assumptions to review and scrutiny, and communicate in a considered way. These steps can be frustrating at times, but ultimately they help leaders apply their best thinking more often. Without an approach of this kind, leaders may start solving the wrong problem, suffer cognitive overload or confuse the team.

For teams, this approach provides clearer context (including goals). It is a way to raise difficult issues safely. It also provides a basis for specific capability development and a foundation for inevitable changes in direction. When leaders make their mental models explicit and create a safe environment for collaboration, capable teams can organise their activities around these models, deliver results and adapt when complexity emerges. This may require additional work at the front end of programs and projects, but it delivers significant benefits.

A network map emerges as work streams are clarified and the interactions between these work streams are crystallised. Across this network, capability and performance can improve steadily, despite ongoing change.

Case Study 5 provides an example of how this approach was applied within a major financial organisation. A network map helped to clarify the role and work of the board and align it with management.

Case Study 5
Defining the role and work of a board and management team

We were asked to help a major financial organisation that had recently been through a successful initial public offering.[59] Both the chairman and the CEO were relatively new in their roles. The chairman wanted to make sure that the company would remain a leader in its industry. His specific objective was to take what he perceived to be a very competent board and management team, which operated relatively independently, and to work with his fellow directors and the CEO to ensure that both these high-performing units were well aligned.

For the chairman's objective to be reached, both the board and management needed to have a clear and shared understanding of the role and work of the board, the role and work of the management team, and the key elements of the interface where the work overlapped.

Working with the chairman, the directors and the CEO, we mapped the work of the board and the senior management team on to two separate hubs and clarified the board–management interface. This produced the model shown in Figure 15. The model helped to focus the board agenda and management's input on their shared work. It also allowed the board and management to discuss who was doing what and highlight improvement areas.

Figure 15. Mapping the work of the board and management

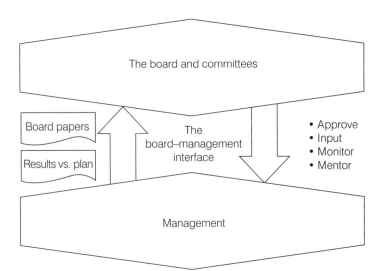

We also created a model that described the strategy work shared by the board and management (Figure 16). This ensured that a common language could be used. The model was used to clarify management's communications to the board and to channel the board's response. It allowed the new management team to better leverage the capabilities of the chairman and directors, giving the latter a greater understanding of the business. It also made transparent assumptions about political, economic and market risk that had not been clear.

Figure 16. Aligning the work of board and management with a common language

How does network-centred leadership work?

As the structured discussion described above plays out repeatedly across an organisation, various network maps will be created. As these maps are shared and integrated, a new way of 'seeing' the work in an organisation emerges.

Traditional management thinking starts by developing goals and strategy. Then structure follows strategy. Finally, the work that needs to be done to execute the strategy is organised in relation to the leaders at the top of the structure.

Enterprise collaboration cuts across hierarchy so that people can 'get things done', despite the hierarchy. People are encouraged to self-organise and act independently. This creates a second stream of work requests, which flow between everybody in the organisation.

Network-centred leadership ensures that these different approaches are aligned. It does this by making all the work that the team, organisation or enterprise needs to do explicit through a single, shared network map.

This 'single version of the truth' helps to ensure that all of the relevant leaders and teams are focused on the same list of valuable work. It helps to identify and manage the complex issues where collaboration is required and separate them from the work streams where traditional approaches remain valid. As importantly, it highlights critical information requirements and provides feedback loops to senior management, who can often become isolated.

Why is it necessary?

Many leaders work hard to align their teams on a periodic basis—at the start of a year, a project or a role. However, they can soon become absorbed by the daily grind of back-to-back meetings and never-ending emails. Over time, the operating environment drifts away from the original plan. Sometimes, they recognise the changes and adjust. But sometimes miscommunications and misdirection occur and a crisis follows.

If leaders regularly invest a small amount of time in robust conversation and maintain a good-quality network map, they can better align people, strategy, markets, work and technology on a *continuous* basis. The value of this improved alignment and transparency increases as the environment becomes more complex and more interconnected.

When the environment is stable, the approach simply confirms the logic and assumptions that support the organisational design.

The structured discussion details what needs to be done by each group and confirms the hierarchical or project leadership techniques to be used. The approach helps to maintain a healthy level of alignment between strategy, organisation and approach. Such small investments over time help to ensure that leadership capability issues are identified early and can be addressed before they become major problems.

The broader value of network-centred leadership emerges when the complexity of the changing environment exceeds the knowledge and processing capacity of any one individual. Here, the challenges of leadership risk, misalignment and cognitive overload destroy enormous amounts of value.

In these situations, network-centred leadership:

- helps leaders to align their strategy and organisation with the dynamic forces that they need to address, especially the potential of new technologies

- supports the wide range of leadership approaches and organisational structures that may need to be used across an enterprise. Specifically, it works successfully with both the formal structure of the organisation and the informal networks being established

- ensures that everybody is clear about what needs to be done, no matter how uncertain the environment or broad the team

- gives permission for individuals and teams to raise issues and ask questions about the evolving environment

- assists leaders to frame their work explicitly, which helps them to make better decisions and avoid cognitive overload

- provides a way for leaders to access help when they don't know what to do to deliver on their targets

- supports and normalises ongoing change so that leaders and organisations can stay aligned to changing markets

- provides a foundation for new social platforms so that new technologies can be used to best effect.

In the next three chapters, we will explore three aspects of network-centred leadership:

- the work streams that make up an enterprise, which can be effectively modelled as a network

- the leadership required to drive each work stream, which is simply an additional kind of work

- the framing of leadership as work, and how leadership approaches can vary and change to meet evolving needs within this framework.

Chapter 9 then synthesises these ideas into a single, coherent approach and summarises the benefits of network-centred leadership.

Chapter 6
Networks can better manage portfolios of work

'It is not the strongest of the species that survives, nor the most intelligent that survives.
It is the one that is the most adaptable to change.'
~ Charles Darwin ~

Everywhere you look, networks are delivering outstanding results in a range of environments. In cyberspace, millions of people have come together to build software, solve problems and create new sources of content. In the natural world, various biological networks, like ant colonies, navigate turbulence and build impressive organisations with only a few simple decision rules. This chapter explains how these adaptive structures can provide an effective way to model work.

Roles are breaking down as a way to manage work

Most organisations use roles and hierarchies to frame work. Hierarchies effectively break work into relatively independent units under the direction of a single leader. When these structures work well, leaders can set priorities, decide methods and select teams based on personal experience or instructions from above. Everyone is then relatively free to do their job, within agreed parameters.

In a hierarchical approach, leaders engage via a particular role, which lays out the work that they are expected to deliver. Information flows and decision rights are 'hardwired' to the hierarchy. Projects and special teams of various types can be used to address gaps.

As discussed in Part 1, this approach is breaking down for three reasons:

1. More of the work requires interconnection between different groups or organisations. Partnerships, problem solving, innovation and deal making are among the various types of collaborative work that are increasingly part of people's work life.

2. Humans are subject to a range of biases that mean they often don't solve the right problems, make the best choices or use the most appropriate methods. As conditions get more difficult, organisations are less able to absorb this underperformance.

3. The 'right' way to do things is becoming increasingly unclear. Complex problems require a range of strategies and options that are beyond the scope of any one person's abilities. In these cases, the leader may not know all the relevant areas of business, or the cause-and-effect relationship between work and the desired goals. To create effective outcomes, collaboration is essential.

A different approach is required

As work becomes more diverse and interconnected, organisations need people to connect directly and appropriately on a wide range of issues. However, this is unlikely to occur organically as teams become more diverse and churn intensifies.

Organisations need a new way to describe the various work streams that are in progress at any one time so that people can collaborate effectively. Everybody needs to have the same 'list'. In addition, they need a shared understanding of what is going on in the broader environment, a language for discussion, and an agreed method to manage change.

Social platforms can provide the desired level of clarity across the whole organisation. Technically, it is as simple as creating a single site with a single list of all the work that needs to be done. But this is insufficient. People typically have different levels of access and different levels of responsibility, depending on the work stream in question.

A new framework is required to collectively describe and deliver a shared list of work—one that specifically defines the context and plans for each work stream.

Networks provide an alternative

Networks provide this single coherent framework. They can be used to organise a portfolio of work and address issues of alignment across a team or a broader organisation.

Each work stream can be modelled as a network node (called a 'hub' in this book). Hubs can represent all kinds of organisational structures, projects, problems, relationships or other issues. Each hub may have different goals, methods and leadership approaches. Links between hubs can be used to represent interconnections between pieces of work. The result is a picture like Figure 17, called a *network map*.

In some cases, the hubs in a network will be aligned to roles in the existing hierarchy. In others, the work will be less structured and leaders, teams and organisations will need to be organised to best meet the needs of the work.

Figure 17. Work modelled as a network of hubs

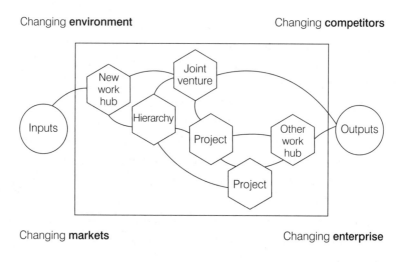

Mapping what needs to be done in this way ensures that each executive in an organisation has a common understanding of the various work streams. It provides a bridge between the hierarchical organisational structure and the free-format activities of social platforms to ensure that the right approach is being used for each piece of work.

Everybody in the organisation has a common point of reference to understand what is going on. They can then work on one or more hubs without interfering with each other.

The value of this approach has been demonstrated by the software industry. In 1985, software development followed the same kind of linear, discrete work paths that many managers follow today.[60] Since then, however, a more distributive method of development has been shown to be considerably more productive. This is variously called agile or object-oriented development (or a range of other names).

Developers have learned how to break problems into relatively independent pieces called objects. The different objects interact with each other through agreed interfaces, creating a network.

They organise people around objects so that groups can work more independently. The network can be maintained despite changing customer requirements and other types of complexity. The approach creates a network organisation with semi-autonomous work groups.[61]

Other kinds of work can be managed in the same way. If capable leaders and teams apply the right lenses or frameworks to a problem, they will be able to break it up into sensible 'chunks'.[62] When the connections (or interfaces) between these chunks are added, it creates a network map.

Each work stream is represented independently of the organisational structure. This allows more considered conversation and better planning, without as many human biases. Executives can discuss and agree on their assumptions about each work stream without reference to particular leaders.

Case Study 6 provides an example of how a leader applied network thinking to the management of an enterprise and addressed issues caused by the use of a matrix structure.

Case Study 6
A change in leadership approach

A new CEO, appointed to lead a global professional services firm, engaged Waypoint. The company had grown by acquisition, before its stock price fell markedly following the global financial crisis of 2007–2008.

In the past, the organisation had been run as a global matrix of functions, geographies and service lines (with nobody below the CEO responsible for profit). The new CEO quickly had to restore financial discipline.

The answer was to change the company's leadership approach and organise the business around approximately 40 hubs, each led by a general manager. This change devolved power to a cohort of general managers, giving each a clear operating scope and profit target (Figure 18).

These 40 leaders were organised into five service lines and given new limits of authority to pursue revenue and profit. There was an agreed delegation of authority. The senior team took responsibility for the various coordination issues so that the general managers could focus on profitable customer service.

The success of this approach relied on the ability of the senior team to delegate real decision rights to the leader at each hub so that they could run their businesses to meet local conditions. The general managers were free to collaborate across functional, geographic and service lines as appropriate. The result was both a stabilisation of the company and the identification of various profit opportunities.

Figure 18. Organisation presented as a network of business units (hubs)

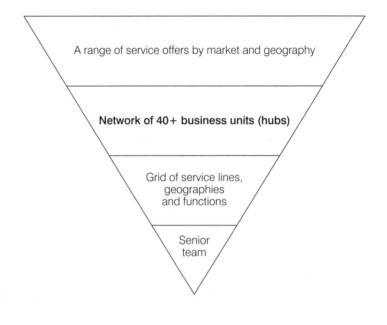

Networks support hierarchies

Network maps provide a complementary way to view organisational structures. They are compatible with a hierarchy as well as alternative organisational forms.[63] For example, an enterprise may consist of:

- a CEO running a conglomerate that supports an industry-wide supply chain

- divisional leaders running various parts of the conglomerate

- business unit leaders sharing common capabilities in a division

- functions or work group leaders working in these businesses

- managers of various kinds, supervisors and various front-line staff.

To run the conglomerate, the CEO works together with the divisional leaders and functional peers as a senior team. The division leader works with the business unit leaders and functional peers to share capabilities across the division, and so on.

Network maps can be applied at each of these different levels of work, or 'altitudes'. Each hub corresponds to somebody's role. Then each hub can be broken down to represent the work of the team below and provide more detail. Equally, each level of the map can be represented as a hub on the layer above. Figure 19.

Figure 19. Networks can represent multiple levels of work

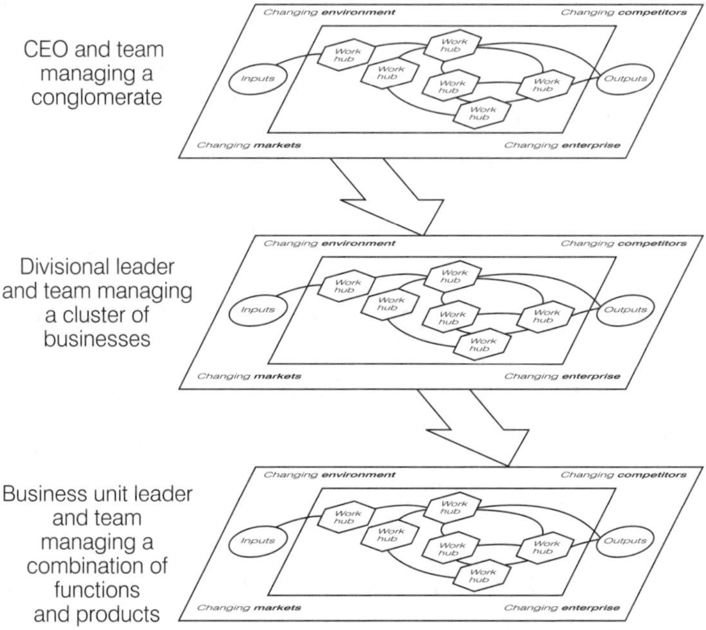

CEO and team managing a conglomerate

Divisional leader and team managing a cluster of businesses

Business unit leader and team managing a combination of functions and products

Network maps can then move beyond the traditional hierarchy. They can be used to reflect projects and cross-functional teams that are working in parallel to solve new problems. Leaders may also want to represent unstructured risks or opportunities. In each case, hubs can simply be added to the network as appropriate. All of the different kinds of work that need to be done are literally on the same page. Collaborative initiatives are aligned with 'business as usual' work.

Network maps support effective communication and learning

A network map provides context for teams without creating information overload. It explains the various kinds of work that are in progress, the status at each hub and the leadership approaches that are being used. With this context, individuals and teams can focus on their hubs and key interfaces to work effectively.

Leaders can describe the different roles that each person plays at each hub. This can all be communicated via a single network map (Figure 20). Without a map of this kind, people can get lost in the sea of information and activity can become unfocused.

Figure 20. Using a network map to provide context

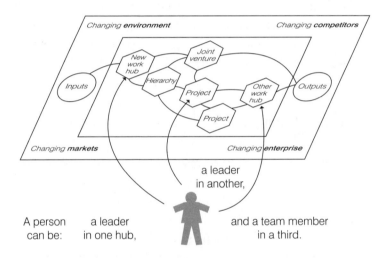

The quality of this kind of approach will obviously vary depending on the quality of the map and its contents. A well-constructed network map has five characteristics:[64]

1. **Efficiency**—To address problems of cognitive overload, any map needs to be easy to understand and use.[65] The map should be simple, so that most team members can

remember it, find it, understand it, and describe it without needing to think too hard.[66]

2. **Coherence**—The various work streams should make sense with respect to each other.[67] Common terms should be used across the network. Interfaces with other groups need to be clear. In practice, this means that the various spreadsheets, presentations, documents and emails flying around all fit together in a coherent way.

3. **Validity**—The map should accurately reflect what needs to be done in real life to achieve the desired business results.[68] Strategies are often described in abstract terms, making it impossible to know exactly what to do to achieve results. The better maps are anchored to what the organisation is trying to achieve through the use of numbers. They provide clear explanations about the work to be completed.

4. **Persuasiveness**—People who use the map, and its related materials, should come away feeling better and clearer about their work, not drained and confused.[69]

5. **Adaptability**—The map should be able to survive change. Repetition and consistency are important to maintain maps so that they remain valuable, despite change.[70]

Networks can facilitate adaption because they are robust

Dynamic and complex environments are not new. In the last few decades, academics have conducted research to better understand various aspects of leadership in these environments. Relevant fields include:

1. complex adaptive systems as a model for major change in environmental science[71] and other domains[72]

2. behavioural economics and psychology, which help to explain how people interact and make decisions under pressure[73]

3. adult learning (including social constructionism and systems thinking)[74]

4. knowledge management (including patterns)

5. alternative organisational structures and management approaches (a range of options exist between hierarchical and agile management approaches).[75]

At a practical level, software developers have for three decades wrestled with the issues of ambiguity, complexity and accelerating cycle times. To accommodate growing complexity, the software industry has tested a wide range of leadership approaches and organisational forms. Internal development teams at Microsoft, for example, were challenged by collaborative networks of volunteers supporting Linux and Firefox.

Both research and practical experience show that networks provide a successful way to model activity. Each network hub represents an agent or team that works relatively independently. Depending on the context, these hubs may represent different business units, project teams, physical or digital capabilities, or soldiers in a battlefield.

These kinds of networks make strategic progress in two ways. Some improve or expand on existing hubs to increase market share or improve performance (exploitation). Others create new hubs to focus on entering new markets or testing new technologies (exploration).

Change can be accommodated by altering the shape of the network, by adding or subtracting hubs, or by changing the work within hubs. Usually, only some of the hubs are affected, leaving most of the agents and teams to continue uninterrupted. This view of the enterprise is independent of individuals. It also does not include particular leadership approaches. Both can be changed at a hub without impacting the integrity of the network.

The right balance between connectivity, flexibility and structure emerges as a result of the interplay between the various hubs at each level of the organisation. Networks can produce effective solutions without the need for extensive supervision because they are guided by relatively simple rules and the use of agreed interfaces.

Network-centred leadership builds on this research and applies it to complex organisations.[76] It can be applied recursively, and at different levels in the organisation, because technically it is self-similar, or fractal.[77]

Work in an enterprise naturally organises into five to seven different levels of ambiguity.[78] Some work may take more time, have larger or more sophisticated outputs, or require more abstract methods than others, but there is an underlying commonality.

If properly constructed, both the structure of hierarchies and the corresponding network maps will align to these layers of increasing ambiguity in an organisation. Each layer of management solves problems and provides context for the layers of management below. The hubs at one level can be decomposed into entire networks at the lower level, with each hub creating a context for the layer below.

In the rest of this book, discussions about a single hub or team can be applied to a whole network and vice versa.[79] Any network can be converted to a single hub by simply 'going up a level of altitude' and putting a ring around the entire network.

Chapter 7
Leadership is just another type of work

'Effective leadership is not about making speeches or being liked;
leadership is defined by results, not attributes.'
~ Peter Drucker ~

If the leader is no longer the person at the top of the hierarchy making decisions based on superior knowledge and experience, then what is a leader supposed to do? What is leadership? This chapter frames the challenge of leadership in complex organisations. It proposes a work-based definition of leadership that is separate from particular individuals and focused on specific outcomes.[80]

Traditional definitions of leadership are insufficient

There are many ways to define leaders and leadership. Commonly, leadership is described as a process of social influence in which one person can enlist the aid and support of others in order to accomplish a common task. According to this definition, a leader is one who shows the way, commands or directs.[81]

This type of definition of leadership implies that a single person leads or commands a group, organisation or country. When viewed through this lens, discussion about leadership is focused on an individual's characteristics, traits, behaviours, styles or capabilities. Or it may be about a person's position in an organisational dynamic, leading to discussions of power and position.[82]

Viewing leadership in terms of personal characteristics, or a person's position in a team or organisation, is a valid approach, but it is insufficient in complex environments. The challenges of the changing environment exceed the knowledge and processing capacity of any one individual and social hierarchies break down.

In complex environments, where a program of work, its context and its leadership are intertwined and dynamic, leadership needs to be treated as a design variable that can be adjusted to meet the demands of the problem at hand. The language and thinking about leadership need to be flexible beyond specific individuals. It is not enough to reorganise work around existing leaders and structures. Leadership capabilities need to be matched dynamically to the evolving work in a more flexible manner.

To do this effectively, leadership needs to be separated from both individuals and organisational structure. The various leadership streams that are required at any one time can then be untangled from the individuals who might provide the leadership. The challenges can be discussed less personally and the control of tasks reallocated more effectively.

Case Study 7 provides an example of a successful leader who failed to adapt to a new environment. It highlights the differences between individual capability, organisational position and work.

Case Study 7
What makes a successful leader?

A major financial institution, wishing to change from being a mutual fund to a listed company, engaged the services of a proven chief executive known for his ability to create value in underperforming organisations. He was so successful in demutualising and listing that the new shareholders found their equity had grown in excess of $7 billion.

At this point he was widely regarded as a model leader. The board decided to extend the CEO's tenure and charged him with the job of profitably growing the business's base internationally. Even though his personal capabilities and his position in charge of a major institution did not change, his context did.

His initial success was achieved by improving operational performance and changing the form of the corporation. He now faced the challenge of leading a listed entity and investing capital to generate growth. This new environment and set of challenges were quite different to anything he had experienced.

Regrettably, these changed circumstances were beyond his particular capabilities. He did not understand the new context and was not open to feedback or advice. The business's momentum faltered and the share price dropped, wiping out a substantial portion of the shareholder gains. Despite two subsequent changes of leader, the company has yet to recover the position it achieved immediately after the initial public offering.

The failure occurred because he and the board focused on the continuity of the role rather than the change in the environment. If they had focused on the work that needed to be done in the new environment, the results may have been very different.

A definition of leadership as work

This book goes beyond individual or role-based definitions of leadership. It defines leadership as the work of organising a group of people to achieve an outcome that may be evolving. This leadership is typically executed by a group of people working to find positive answers to our four questions on an ongoing basis:

1. Have we clearly **defined** our context?

2. Are we **designing** effective plans and solutions?

3. Have we **developed** capable teams?

4. Are we **delivering** target performance?

Millions of people, at various levels of organisations around the world, are grappling with these questions.[83] They are in different kinds of organisations, have different personal capabilities and have different amounts of power and influence, but they are all being asked to lead teams and deliver outcomes, despite ongoing change.

All of these people are leaders because they:

1. **define** and analyse the environment, clarify goals and governance limits and turn ad hoc ideas into strategies. This establishes a shared frame of reference in which communities can work.

2. **design** and agree upon the composition of teams and methods to be used to execute the strategies and achieve the goals. This may range from traditional hierarchies executing set processes, to loose-knit teams exploring a new market or technology. In more uncertain environments, teams may need to consider alternatives, develop and test a range of options, and learn lessons before a valid plan or solution emerges.

3. **develop** individuals and teams so that they have the requisite capabilities to be successful. This requires that people be developed to perform today's work and to have longer term career paths to meet the future needs of the organisation.

4. **deliver** against an agreed performance management framework. Typically, this occurs through an agreed set of communication and decision-making protocols.

The four kinds of leadership work can be represented as a cycle (Figure 21).

Figure 21. Leadership as a cycle of four kinds of work

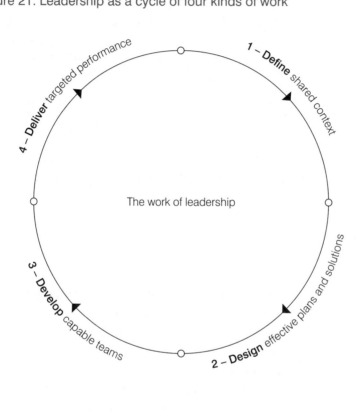

An organisation is likely to have a wide portfolio of leadership work streams in progress at any one time. These may be at different 'altitudes' and states of maturity. For example, work streams may include:

- a leader running an organisation, creating and assigning strategic programs

- a project manager delivering on a specific set of goals

- a team member assigned to a specific activity.

The work-based definition of leadership is appropriate in all of these situations. It can be applied recursively, and at different levels, in the organisation. Like networks, it is self-similar or fractal (that is, it has similar characteristics, irrespective of the scale). Finally, it should be regarded as an aid to judgement and not as a process or method.

Case Study 8 is a good example of how one company dealt with a changing context by including a range of people in the leadership process and cycling through the work. They navigated four separate transformational stages, raising performance standards at each stage and almost doubling shareholder value in three years.

Case Study 8
Doubling shareholder value in a changing environment

When the new chairman and CEO started at a client organisation from the transport sector, they inherited an underperforming government business enterprise. But over time, it has been transformed into a successful, publicly listed enterprise with strong growth prospects.

To make the transformation happen, the company has been led through four distinct stages over approximately five years (Figure 22). At each stage of the journey, the context of the organisation changed. The approach and capabilities that were required were varied in order to suit the task at hand.

At each point of inflection, the CEO and his team worked with the board to define the new situation, design a way forward, develop appropriate capabilities and deliver results for the stakeholders. Many people, both line managers and their staff, played leadership roles in the company's transformation. The result has been a near doubling in share price since the initial public offering.

Figure 22. A four-stage strategic journey

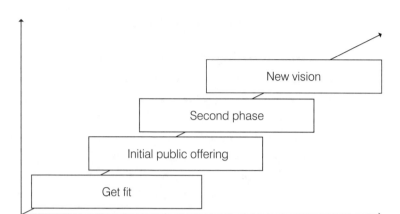

- Stage 1—Operational improvement, which focused on getting the company fit enough to provide the state government shareholder with some options, namely to sell all or part of the enterprise to a private buyer, to have an initial public offering, or to restructure.

- Stage 2—An initial public offering, which implemented the government's preferred option to float the company on the national exchange.

- Stage 3—Second-phase operational improvement, which involved further restructuring and improving the capability of the organisation to deliver on the promises in the initial public offering prospectus and to chart a course to world-class operating performance.

- Stage 4—Exploring growth options, which focused on identifying and locking in game-changing growth opportunities for the enterprise, while building parallel capabilities.

Implications of work as a definition of leadership

Framing leadership as work has a number of implications:

1. **Leadership is distributed**. Many people in an organisation are working as leaders, at different levels of ambiguity and in different domains of expertise. This is particularly true when the relationship between cause and effect is unclear or dynamic. In these situations, any leader is unlikely to know exactly what to do and will need the help of a coalition of people. By implication, an individual is not inherently a 'good' or 'bad' leader. They may excel at the leadership work required in one sphere of influence or period of time, but be less effective in others.

2. **Leadership is not bound by the organisation**. Sometimes, leadership work occurs within an organisation. However, increasingly it is occurring in collaboration with partners, suppliers, and clients and customers.

3. **Leadership work can be managed like any other work**. Much of leadership has been made to seem mysterious or unknowable because of a lack of transparency and discussion. If it is viewed simply as a specific type of work, then it can be managed using conventional work management approaches. Defining the work of leadership leads naturally to a broader conversation about work clarity.

4. **Context matters**. To be effective, leaders need to understand the context that frames their work. They need to understand the scope of their role or their team's role, the forces that influence its shape, and the priorities and the goals that define success. Clarifying this context gives leaders and team members far more freedom to work creatively and independently.

5. **Work methods are context specific.** The best way to complete a particular piece of leadership work will depend on the specific context and capabilities of the team that is engaged to do the task. A corollary to this is that leadership capability and development can only be properly described in a particular context. Generic role profiles and theoretical models of capability break down badly at the senior executive level because there is considerable freedom, which can affect any role or context.

6. **The 'right' leadership style and behaviours are situational and team dependent.** Prescriptions about universally appropriate styles or behaviours fail to properly reflect the diversity of the situations in which people find themselves. Each leader and team should be encouraged to define the behaviours that are right for them in their context, and to stick rigorously to those behaviours. The overarching style of working and set of behaviours that a team agrees on is more important than the particular approach they choose to adopt in different situations.

Practical benefits of work as a definition of leadership

There are a number of reasons why the definition of leadership as work is useful in practice:

- **Work is tangible.** Most leaders have a language to describe what they are working on, and are willing to discuss the work that they are doing. They may not be able to articulate the strategy or goals to which they are contributing, but they can usually describe their work with great granularity and credibility.

- **Work has a clear relationship to outcomes**. Much leadership discussion drifts into a range of second- and third-order factors that may influence performance. Ensuring that people are doing both the right leadership work and the right work of other kinds directly contributes to outcomes.

- **Work exposes context safely**. Talking about work implies goals, assumptions and context without judging. Differences between mental models can then be examined and discussed with the team. Discussing context from this safe position helps to alleviate some of the social issues associated with collaboration and change.

- **Work is usually shared**. While some critical work, and decisions, must be undertaken by an individual, most executive work involves many people. Talking about work encourages alignment and collaboration.[84]

- **Work is not personal**. Work is what people do, not what people are. It can be discussed and changed with less offence and resistance than, say, organisational structure or individual roles. When a description of work is written down, it provides a safe point of reference for broader, ongoing discussion.

- **Work is flexible**. Work is a very flexible idea. A wide variety of processes, methods and approaches fit comfortably under the umbrella of work. Work also travels comfortably at different altitudes in an organisation. Talking about work allows discussion between any two people without presupposing a hierarchy, method or approach.

- **Work is expected**. People are expected to know what work they are doing and to feel like they ought to be able to describe it. It is not acceptable for people to say that they won't discuss their work, even when they are new to a role.

Chapter 8
Leadership work can be performed in a variety of ways

'Fit no stereotypes. Don't chase the latest management fads.
The situation dictates which approach best accomplishes
the team's mission.'
~ Colin Powell ~

Some books on leadership suggest that there is one 'right' way to lead. This is not one of them. The range of challenges that leaders face is so broad and complex, it is folly to pretend that there is a single answer. Instead, we think of various leadership approaches as 'clubs in a golf bag'. Each is useful in certain situations.

Most leaders will be familiar with traditional hierarchical leadership and project leadership. They may also be aware of collaborative leadership approaches. This chapter reviews these three approaches to represent the spectrum of alternatives available to today's leaders. It focuses on collaboration, which is hard and less well understood, yet increasingly necessary.

The challenge that leaders face is to be able to pick the right 'club' in each situation. Network-centred leadership frames each approach in terms of the work of leadership, shown in Figure 23. With this common language, the different leadership approaches become interchangeable options that leaders can use as required.

Figure 23. Different leadership approaches framed as work

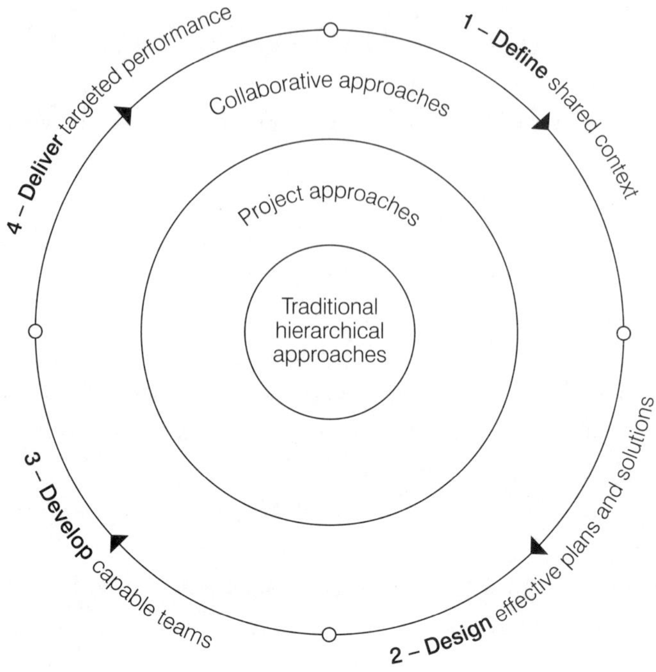

A summary of hierarchical and project leadership approaches

Hierarchical and project leadership approaches provide a point of departure for this discussion of leadership. We assume that both these approaches are familiar to readers. They can be used to illustrate the four kinds of leadership work described in the previous chapter.

In both these approaches, the leader is usually somebody who has come up through the ranks and performed many of the roles in the hierarchy or team. They can provide specific direction because they are expert in many of the disciplines relevant to the team or organisation.

Traditional hierarchical leadership

Organisational hierarchy has been an effective organisation form for hundreds of years. Well-established hierarchical leadership approaches, which derive from the military, have evolved to successfully provide a clear frame of reference for executive work.

In hierarchies, the locus of power is at the top. Leaders usually know what to do and can communicate their approach to the team through 'command and control' protocols. Planning and budgeting are typically managed on a yearly and five-yearly basis. Goals and initiatives are deployed through a cascade of communication from one layer of the hierarchy down to the next. Communication occurs in meetings. Reports and processes confirm performance and provide any clarification that is needed. As time goes by, instructions are executed, real outcomes are achieved and the approach is refined.

Messages can become distorted, but the structure is usually well established, systems are stable and the vision is well understood, so results are usually achieved. Also, hierarchies have evolved to shorten the lines of communication as competitive conditions have become more intense. For example, Andrew Liveris, chief executive of the Dow Chemical Company, has commented that there are now only six layers between him and entry-level positions in the company, improving communication.[85]

While flatter structures bring leaders closer to the 'trenches', they also mean that the span of leadership has widened. In markets that are stable, the hierarchical approach for the most part retains its efficacy. However, when complexity emerges, there are fewer 'managers managing managers' available to find new solutions.

Figure 24 illustrates a typical hierarchical structure.

Figure 24. A typical hierarchy

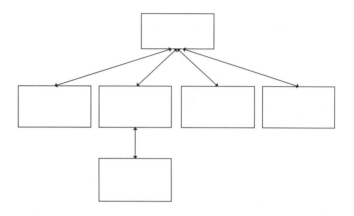

Project leadership

Project-based leadership approaches are also well understood. Teams form around a particular project scope, or charter, and operate independently of traditional hierarchies. Project plans, timelines and budgets are used to create context for the team. Work is characterised by work breakdown structures and project roles. Again, these techniques are well established. They will remain a significant part of any leadership toolkit in the future.

Projects provide a more flexible way of achieving specific outcomes because there tends to be less concern with long-term power relationships than is the case within hierarchies. Projects are, by their nature, temporary. They entail the creation of a temporary organisation to deliver a set of time-sensitive and specific outcomes (Figure 25). Project teams can work within, or across, organisations to accomplish particular tasks under time constraints.

Figure 25. A typical project

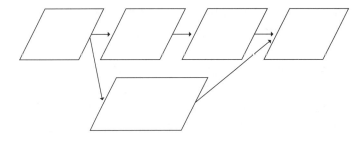

Projects are used regularly to augment hierarchies by providing cross-functional and expert teams of various kinds. Sales and political projects can be used to align interests and create deals. Technical projects can be used to manage complicated and complex technical challenges like capital works, new system implementations, or cross-functional improvement initiatives. If leaders assemble the relevant skills and capabilities, they will be able to use established project methods to deliver desired results.

Collaborative leadership

Collaborative leadership is designed for environments where no one person has the power to take a unilateral decision, either because no hierarchical structure is practical or because no individual knows enough to tell others what to do. Instead, people, teams or organisations choose to cooperate to find a way forward.

This kind of leadership is often required to create new growth opportunities. Finding effective new solutions and methods requires a 'search for some kind of harmony between two intangibles: a form which we have not yet designed and a context which we cannot properly describe'.[86] This usually requires a process of iteration. Leaders and teams move forward using the best information that they have, but this activity generates new information about the environment and highlights new issues and opportunities. Teams learn and then adjust plans rapidly based on feedback. To be effective, this process requires transparency, clear communication and structured learning (collectively creating a 'learning organisation').[87]

Collaboration, supported by social platforms, is becoming a major source of competitive advantage for many enterprises. A wide range of online communities can now help to provide both ideas and services to organisations. Leaders and organisations that cannot adapt are likely to be beaten in the marketplace.

A typical collaborative environment is represented visually in Figure 26.

Figure 26. A typical collaborative solution occurs iteratively

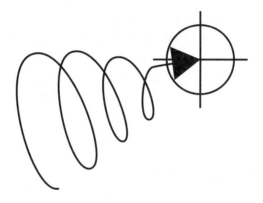

It is not hard to understand why senior executives may find collaborative leadership psychologically difficult. They are not used to the lack of control it entails,[88] or to the different types of relationships that it implies. More broadly, individuals who are used to a privileged position because of access to information are not going to like enterprise collaboration.

To be a successful collaborator, leaders need to expose their capabilities, assumptions and mental models to scrutiny. They need to be secure enough to allow their peers and team to critique those assumptions. In a hierarchy or project, there is simply no good reason for leaders to take that kind of personal risk. It is much safer to control information flows and decision rights and then manage any gaps and disagreements that emerge in private, one-on-one discussions.

At some point, most leaders will find that they have to deal with this more transparent and inclusive approach. In complex environments, they don't have a choice. Complexity has reduced a leader's ability to know the right way forward. If they repeatedly try, and fail, to provide sensible direction, their credibility will suffer. If leaders try to control all aspects of the work, as they might do in a hierarchy or project, they are doomed to the life of Sisyphus in Greek mythology: rolling an immense boulder up a hill every day, only to watch it roll down again when circumstances change.

To understand how collaborative leadership works, we will consider how it answers our four leadership questions.

1. Defining clear context collaboratively

Collaborative teams operating in complex environments may not be clear about what needs to be done to create value. The first step is to bring people together to share information and build a consensus about the situation, current activity and potential goals.

A collaborative leader needs to build a coalition that has people with the requisite capabilities and create a sense of psychological safety so that everybody will engage in the process.

To illustrate the significance of this type of leadership change, remember how production work changed in the total quality management era two generations ago. Initially, a manager supervised and instructed production workers directly. Then quality initiatives and enterprise systems were introduced, giving everybody on the shop floor access to the same information and permission to discuss changes and take actions independently.

Complex environments force leaders to do the same thing, but with higher order leadership work. We recommend using a network map to facilitate and structure this discussion, but a range of methods are available to combine the various perspectives.

2. Designing effective plans and solutions collaboratively

Once a work stream has been defined, leaders will typically test a number of options to find the most valuable combinations of strategy, people and technology.[89] They have little choice because nobody knows a priori what will work best, or how events might unfold. As teams go along, they learn to sense what is happening in the environment, and then respond accordingly.

A range of planning techniques have emerged to help teams prepare for, and test, various scenarios. They create plans that are better described as a range of trials, options and initiatives.[90] Teams can decide between these options in real time, depending on circumstances, so creating, juggling and then implementing these various choices becomes a real-time activity. It typically requires the input and contribution of a range of people from different levels and parts of an organisation.

3. Developing capable teams collaboratively

Learning is a critical component of a collaborative approach. It is not a separate activity, but rather an integrated part of a recursive process.

Leaders and teams start building capability and executing a plan. Over time, new information emerges, people learn about the new environment, and the focus and mix of work streams organically change. Leaders and teams have to go back and confirm their assumptions and refine their approach. This can feel like doing the same thing over and over again, but there is little choice when the environment keeps changing.

The challenge is not getting people to learn—everybody wants to learn. It is finding senior leaders and teams who are willing and able to structure trials and projects to provide valuable insights about the environment and then share the results. When teams discuss this information in a safe environment, learning can occur rapidly.

4. Delivering results collaboratively

In collaborative environments, people complete tasks that are allocated dynamically between team members. If properly designed, work moves dynamically between team members to meet the needs of evolving problems and changing environments.[91]

Leaders of a collaborative process are more like a sports coach. In some cases, they are a technical expert and can contribute to the leadership function. In others, they cannot. At a minimum, they should be able to engage others who hold critical subject-matter expertise and steer the team along. They do this by knowing whose judgement to trust for each key decision.

Summary of the three leadership approaches

The different leadership approaches described in this chapter are likely to all be useful at different times. In many cases, traditional hierarchical or project approaches may provide an effective, simple and cheap option. But collaboration is likely to be necessary at critical times, often when the firm is in real danger and new solutions are required. Returning to the analogy of clubs in a golf bag, collaborative leadership is like the sand wedge: the best way to get out of a complex trap.

Table 2 compares the work of the three different leadership approaches. Depending on the environment, any one of these approaches may be most appropriate.

Table 2. Comparison of traditional, project and collaborative leadership approaches

Type of leadership work		Leadership approach		
		Traditional	Project	Collaborative
Define	Frame of reference:	Hierarchy	Project	Iteration
	Strategy and goals are described via:	One- and five-year plans and budgets	Project scope or charter, plans, timelines and budgets	Mission, scenarios and forecasts with assumptions
Design	Work is described by:	Plans, processes and job descriptions	Work breakdown structures	Trials, experiments and pilots
	People engage through:	Roles in a hierarchy	Project roles	Dialogue
Develop	Career progress is:	Linear	Via cohorts	Via a portfolio of work
	Capability development is:	Via roles and processes	Via project needs	Experiential
Deliver	Communication and decision-making protocols are:	Command and control	Project team rules	Group decision-making principles
	Performance is managed via:	Traditional measures, e.g. revenue, people	Project scorecard	Comparison to a model or scenario

Chapter 9
Network-centred leadership in action

'I do not pretend to start with precise questions. I do not think you can start with anything precise. You have to achieve such precision as you can, as you go along.'
~ Bertrand Russell ~

The premise of this book is that if leaders stop and ask four simple questions before, during and after each piece of work, they will be more able to select the right leadership approach and engage in an effective way. If they discuss these questions consistently with those around them and explicitly record their position, they will be more able to align teams across the organisation and succeed in a dynamic environment.

Everybody can answer the four questions to some degree. The question is how well, and how consistently, the team can explain the answers. The challenge is to discuss each question regularly enough, and with sufficient rigour, to ensure that a shared approach becomes instinctive. When the environment becomes challenging, leaders have the habits and practices they need to maintain real team engagement and gain the best thinking available.

A single coherent picture of the work that needs to be done

As the four questions are asked and answered across a range of work streams, a network map emerges that helps to identify everything a team or organisation needs to do to be successful. It describes each work stream, the interactions between them and the leadership approach that is being used for each. Figure 27 provides an example of a network map where a team is managing six hubs and various work streams to create value.

Figure 27. The work of a team as a network map

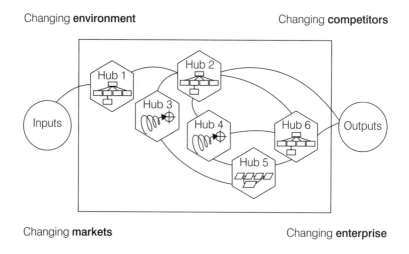

Leaders in this example use traditional leadership approaches to drive operational performance, financial discipline and compliance (in Figure 27, hubs 1, 2 and 6 are run as hierarchies). In addition, they use collaborative approaches to enter new markets and generate growth (hubs 3 and 4). Finally, they will use a project leadership approach to achieve a particular objective (hub 5).

By using a network map, and consistent language, people can better understand and discuss why the organisation has been set up in a particular way. It helps people to understand the different context for each part of the organisation. The additional discussion also creates a psychologically safe place for teams to raise difficult issues when change emerges.

Each hub provides a basis for structured learning and knowledge management. Everybody inside and outside the team can understand the goals of each piece of work and the methods being used, even during periods of change. This helps to avoid confusion when different parts of the organisation are adopting different approaches, or are changing their approaches to adapt to new conditions. Social platforms can be aligned to support each work stream as appropriate.

Leaders can see when they should drive ahead and when they have no special position or information advantage. It alerts them to situations where the nature of control has changed profoundly and a heightened level of self-awareness is required. Once this is achieved, leaders are more able to cede control effectively and engage collaboratively.

A focus on critical work and performance

The purpose of clarifying the work is to better create value. Ideally, everybody's work is aligned to the network map and the map is aligned to the economic and strategic goals of the company. Well-understood work processes can be executed efficiently. Collaboration, creativity and innovation can be applied to the points of greatest leverage for the organisation. Activity and information on social platforms can become more than random chatter.

Once the work has been made transparent, driver trees can be used to expose the relationship between the financial and strategic goals that the company wants to achieve and the work that the people in the company are actually doing. The driver trees can include hindsight (historical results), foresight (forecasts) and insight (key work levels and changes). Figure 28 provides an example of how a driver tree might link the work streams from our network map (Figure 27) through to economic return.

Figure 28. Driver tree as a framework for reporting financial performance

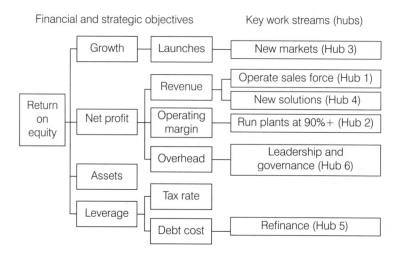

One Waypoint client in the aluminium industry used driver trees that cascaded down through the refinery's operations to relate specific actions to their impact on profitability. For example, the maintenance fitter responsible for the caustic pumps could estimate both the cost in lost caustic of not changing a leaking gland packing and the consequential impact on production should the pump fail. Coupled with an incentive program tied to profitable production tonnes, this had a material impact on plant efficiency.

Network-centred leadership is not a capital-T 'Transformation' that needs to be implemented from above. Rather, it is a safe and effective way to discuss, clarify and optimise what is happening in the organisation today. It recognises that in an increasingly complex world, nobody really has a complete picture of what is going on. Most people in the organisation can't relate to financial statements and strategic plans. They need a more tangible representation of what needs to be done. Equally, senior managers can't personally control what is going on. They need to be able to delegate 'chunks' of work while retaining reasonable visibility, control and governance. Properly structured hubs can achieve both of these objectives.

Implementation is incremental and iterative. While it regularly takes weeks and months to expose and clarify the cause-and-effect relationships between strategy, work, people and outcomes, making these linkages explicit can dramatically improve performance.

When change occurs in the environment, leaders and teams have a network map to identify the hubs that are impacted by a change. They can prioritise the critical work and set a new course for the business in a matter of months, not years. Because there is a 'single version of the truth', the entire team can know what is critical. Due regard can be paid to leaders who are focusing on a critical change project and may be finding it difficult to engage in business as usual.

A framework to develop superior leaders

Senior leaders perform a wide range of work, but only some of this work has the potential to significantly impact the performance of the organisation at any point in time. They can create more value, and avoid cognitive overload, if they can stay focused on this critical work as the environment evolves.

Below the level of the senior team, cohorts of leaders and experts can also perform critical work that contributes disproportionately to the success of the organisation. Examples include traders, fashion buyers, investors, investment managers and designers. Critical work may also occur in a range of other roles, at different points in time. For example, an HR leader's work will become critical during a period when the board is replacing the CEO and many of the top 20 executives. Once the restructure is complete, however, the role will return to its traditional level of importance.

The performance of people leading this critical work has a material impact on the overall success of the enterprise. Small differences in judgement can be the difference between success and failure. The challenge for organisations is to find people who can excel at this critical work and create meaningful advantage for the corporation.

Network-centred leadership is designed to support these competent leaders and critical cohorts. The goal is to create leaders who can perform the critical work of the organisation at a 'very competent' or 'superior' level (the top 16% of performers). This focus helps to ensure that leadership development produces a material economic return for the firm (Figure 29).[92]

Figure 29. Distribution of leadership competence in a general population

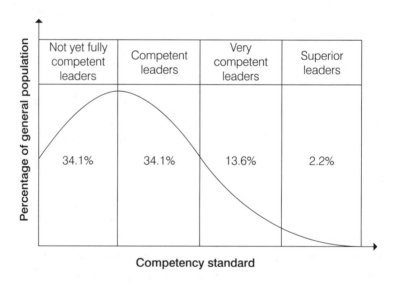

Almost by definition, the people doing critical work have above-average capabilities. They have ascended to positions of seniority and expertise because they possess a range of skills and personal attributes that are outside the normal range (usually including a healthy ego). They also have corresponding weaknesses.

To make improvements at this high level of competence, leaders need to focus on the gaps between the individual's skills and attributes, the requirements of the work, and the approaches they are using. Some of these gaps can be addressed with general training. However, some critical gaps cannot be identified in advance. They emerge only as specific work requirements and team capabilities become clear.

Case Study 9 demonstrates how closely analysing the required work helped a new CEO transition from a functional specialist to an outstanding leader who was able to deliver extraordinary results.

Case Study 9
Helping a competent functional leader become an outstanding CEO

Our client, a financial services administration firm, wanted to transition an individual from the position of senior functional leader to CEO within six months.

The new appointee was a competent and capable functional leader who would score well on most standardised tests. However, she had little previous general management experience.

By analysing the work of the role, we were able to identify the small number of key skills that were going to be essential for the successful execution of the company's strategy. A bespoke development plan was created to focus on these skills. It included formal training via a Harvard Business School short course for general managers to close some of the individual's skills gaps, as well as individual development work to frame her first 100 days in the new role.

A network-centred leadership approach helped her to focus her limited development time on the most critical aspects of her role and then apply her knowledge and skills effectively.

She went on to create a clear vision and align the executive team successfully around the work necessary to achieve her vision. The outcome was a spectacular turnaround. The company went from a loss to a significant profit in 18 months. She has subsequently been recruited to lead an organisation several times the size and scope of the previous one.

A basis for the effective use of social platforms

Social platforms need to do more than simply increase communication to create enterprise value. They need to facilitate the precise kinds of collaboration that are most likely to be valuable for the enterprise. Only by addressing the right issues can a team gain the full benefits of a social platform and perform optimally.

A network map provides the missing context and direction that social platforms need to be effective. It helps each team understand how to best use a social platform to create value and minimise distraction. Specifically, a network map provides:

- **a clear purpose for each team**. Once the work and goals of a hub are clearly defined, it becomes easy to see where collaboration is likely to provide the greatest value. A network map also helps to clarify the kind of social platform that is likely to be most valuable.

- **a basis for psychological safety**. Small groups at each hub are more likely to feel safe with each other and are hence more likely to accept the use of a transparent online environment.

- **agreed work methods**. By clarifying the methods being used at each hub, people know what to do with the new tools in order to be effective. Without this, the technology is only a toolkit.

- **appropriate information and administrative rights**. Different people need different levels of access and control across the enterprise. This is typically achieved in social platforms via technical roles. Implicit in these role allocations is a set of assumptions about who will do what to progress each piece of work. Unless the various hubs have been properly defined, there is no sensible basis to ensure that the people at each hub have the capabilities they need to be successful.

- **a basis to filter information flows**. Social platforms produce a large amount of information, some of which is highly valuable. If everybody has access to every information stream, the valuable signals may be swamped by additional noise. The network map provides a way to filter the information flowing to each hub, putting it into an appropriate context.

- **a framework for feedback and learning**. At each hub, the relationship between business performance and social platform activity is closely aligned. If used effectively, information sourced from social platforms can accelerate learning.

The work of network-centred leadership

Network-centred leadership should be considered as a common starting point for each work stream. It can then evolve into a variety of leadership approaches as required by the particular circumstance. When the environment changes, or a leader suffers from cognitive overload, the team can return to the network-centred leadership approach and reset their direction and approach as required.

The key is to keep returning to each of the four questions and answering them in a consistent way.

1. Defining clear context

Because of the potential for complexity, leaders should start with a collaborative approach. By taking the time to confirm that people are clear and aligned about what needs to be done to create value, they protect themselves from risk. Leaders and teams can do this by bringing communities together to analyse the environment, clarify goals and turn ad hoc ideas into shared context.

Any number of lenses can be used to identify the work that needs to be done. The various work streams can then be represented by a network of hubs. The goal is to allow teams to work at each hub in relative isolation and to interact via relatively clear interfaces.

The network map that is created supports decentralised decision making and enhances communication across a team. Clear documentation of boundaries and expected behaviours provides a foundation for communication at the hubs, and across the interfaces. It helps to ensure that everybody knows enough about what is going on to contribute effectively.

2. Designing effective plans and solutions

Once a work stream has been defined, everybody on the team can contribute to selecting the right way to proceed. Each hub may need a different leadership approach and team structure, ranging from traditional hierarchies to loose-knit teams. Collaboration at this point helps to expose assumptions and ideas for review and clarification. By working in this more open and deliberate manner, the right leadership approaches can be applied and performance materially improved.

Collaboration generates options, elicits the best ideas that everybody has to offer, and ensures that everybody has clear information flows and decision rights. When social platforms are used well, successful patterns can be found and reapplied across hubs to create an enduring advantage. Proper work design also creates a foundation for learning at the hub and across the organisation.[93]

Importantly, collaboration helps prepare people for the changes that are likely to occur. By recognising the potential uncertainty in advance, and creating a psychologically safe environment for discussion, leaders can prepare people to learn and adapt effectively if it becomes necessary.

Leaders may still want to use their own expertise and preferred methods, but the potential for complexity means that at a minimum these should be exposed to the group for scrutiny. Even if leaders don't want to take this step, the increased use of social platforms may force their hand. When these platforms are heavily used, they can quickly become the de facto system of record. They expose context and raise questions, despite what the leader wants.

3. Developing capable teams

If the work of the team or organisation has been explicitly framed as a network and a team is collaborating safely at each hub, then leaders have a range of options to close gaps between the capabilities of an individual, or team, and those capabilities required to do the work. Gap-closing efforts may range from incremental development 'on the job', to more significant capability development supported by the human resource function.

Rather than thinking about capability as a static hierarchy of roles, the network map provides the basis for a much more flexible approach to capability and development. Individuals can be added to, or help at, a particular hub, regardless of the formal roles and hierarchy.

As people work at a hub, they will contribute to, and learn from, the knowledge created at that hub. Leaders can discuss the specific context and teach the appropriate work methods to each team, rather than assuming that people know what is going on. A variety of techniques—including stories, patterns and discussion—can be used to capture and share knowledge about particular problems or situations in their appropriate context.[94]

Once hubs are well established, skills, behaviours and judgement can all be tested in real-world conditions to ensure effectiveness. This allows leaders to delegate authority and manage risk more effectively.

Managing capability across a range of different hubs can be challenging at the organisational level. If companies are to be globally competitive, they must learn to identify and manage the elite individuals who can provide differentiated capabilities. However, there are also powerful reasons why people need to be treated consistently across an organisation as a basis for teamwork and trust.

Professional sports have wrestled with this challenge for decades. They create a team vision and ethos, but in parallel they use data to quantify the specific value of each player on the team. These so-called 'moneyball' techniques are making their way into leadership development.[95] Without an approach of this kind, attracting, retaining and developing a competent team will become an ongoing challenge. The market value of high-performing people is becoming increasingly transparent.

Focusing on work helps leaders identify those parts that are critical and explain why some work and individuals are treated differently. When there is a well-developed understanding of what needs to be done, and how people doing each kind of work need to be managed from a human resource perspective, capability development will have a firm foundation and is likely to be successful.

4. Delivering results

Various hubs across an organisation are likely to deliver results in different ways. Typically, most will continue to use traditional approaches. Increasingly, the most significant value will come from the few iterative, collaborative hubs where innovation is taking place. By framing leadership as a network of hubs, taking the trouble to distribute decision making, and building a wider leadership group, it is possible to identify and prioritise these few critical hubs and put them in context for the rest of the organisation.

Delegating allows others to manage much of the leadership work, within agreed bounds. It leaves time for the leader to scan the external environment and identify emerging trends. In the military, this is called a 'sense and respond' approach.[96]

If leaders are externally focused and dynamic, they can observe points of achievement, failure and discontinuity. This situational awareness helps leaders identify and respond to issues proactively. They can then adjust their responses by repeating the four steps of the network-centred leadership approach at one or more hubs.

Leaders can also respond by moving resources to expand or contract hubs as appropriate. They can initiate new hubs and close down redundant work streams. Teams can adjust to the new work in real time without the need for a formal top-down restructuring. At each hub, the relevant leaders can respond without tripping over their peers. Interfaces have been clearly defined.

An overall picture of the network-centred leadership approach is shown in Figure 30. Each of the four questions of network-centred leadership is discussed in more detail in Part 3.

Figure 30. The work of network-centred leadership

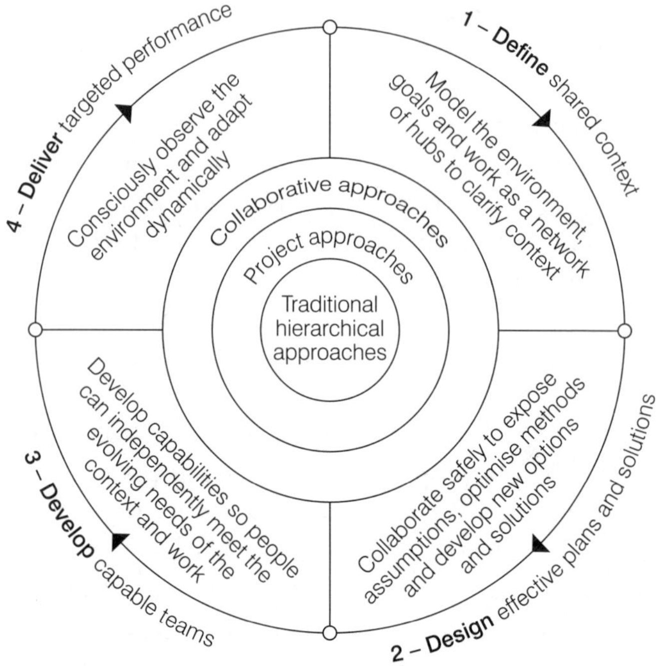

Case Study 10 illustrates how an explicit model that is focused on work can provide a basis for shared knowledge and significant performance improvement.

Case Study 10

Building capability and shared knowledge to improve performance

When we started work with a major contractor, its business consisted of two multi-decade, multibillion-dollar programs that operated independently within a loose corporate structure. The new CEO's challenge was to get the business 'fit' so that it could successfully deliver the two current programs and win future work.

To be successful, the company needed to improve corporate capability, increase collaboration and better share resources between the two current programs. He created a map of the work as a foundation for this development.

The map shown in Figure 31 describes the matrix structure of business units and shared capabilities. It provided a common point of reference for everybody in the executive team as they worked to:

1. **document a complete and shared description of the various capabilities of the organisation**. These were aligned to the roles and teams of the capability general managers. This reduced duplication and gaps between the various general managers and also reduced confusion.

2. **clarify the relationships between those carrying out the program and their capability peers**. This addressed the decision rights of the various general managers. It also framed the interactions between the team members.

3. **develop capability development plans**, which allocated capital to meet the current needs of the program general managers and the future capability requirements of the broader organisation.

The map has been refined through a couple of annual cycles. It is now a part of the shared context of the organisation.

Figure 31. Integration of business programs

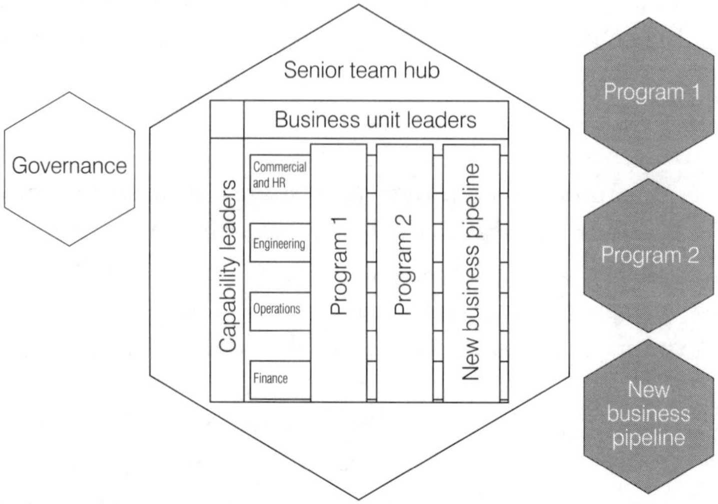

Benefits of network-centred leadership

Given the scale of many strategy programs, even small changes in the performance of leaders and teams can have a significant impact on the performance of an organisation. An investment in network-centred leadership can reduce the business risks of a program and help to capture the 30% of potential value that is typically lost during the execution of strategic initiatives.

Case studies show that leaders who practise network-centred leadership typically improve performance in a number of ways. The benefits usually compound over time. Figure 32 illustrates the kind of difference that network-centred leadership might make by shifting the performance trajectory of a leader and team.

Figure 32. Potential impact of network-centred leadership on performance

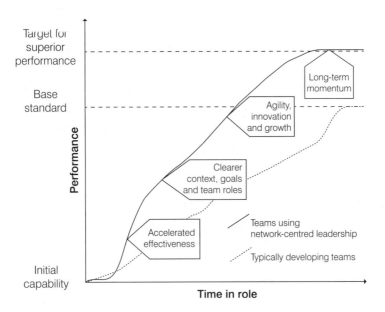

The key benefits of a network-centred leadership approach are:

- **accelerated effectiveness**—If a leader can establish and enforce clear 'non-negotiables', communicate openly and effectively, and demonstrate competence at the beginning of his or her appointment, the group is far more likely to trust and support that executive.[97] By contrast, it is hard for leaders who start off on the wrong foot to recover.

- **clearer context, goals and team roles**—Leaders who can explain the assumptions that they are making to their peers and teams are in a position to improve the quality and rigour of discussion. The team can reframe and refine the analysis of issues and help to ensure that the right types of leadership capability are in place for each program of work.

Explicitly describing the overall work that needs to be done, and the piece that each team has to resolve, improves alignment because it identifies and defines the interfaces. Work that is clear and properly structured to fit the capabilities of the team improves engagement and productivity.[98]

Such additional planning also helps to 'fireproof' leaders and programs against problems of misalignment when changes occur. Like preventative maintenance, going to the dentist or regular exercise, it may not be urgent. But it is usually important.

- **better agility, innovation and growth**—When change inevitably occurs, having a common framework and language helps everybody to discuss and understand what is happening and to contribute appropriately. As issues and ideas come up during discussions, they can be addressed to improve the overall approach. Opportunities for improvement and growth can be identified and captured. Specific gaps in the skills and context of the team can be identified and closed.

- **stronger long-term momentum**—Initially, the network-centred leadership approach may feel hard and 'clunky'; but these small investments help leaders to remain at the right altitude (that is, the right level of abstraction) and use their best thinking during periods of turbulence. It builds consistent, reflexive behaviour, which in turn significantly improves performance and reduces risks for individuals, teams and organisations.

Creating consistent behaviours and a pattern of ongoing success builds trust and momentum. The difference between high versus average performance is significant over time.

Survey

Before reading Part 3, we recommend that you complete the simple survey on the following page to understand how network-centred leadership can help you in a specific work context.

Pick a team that you lead and answer each of the 12 questions with a score of between 0 and 5. Calculate your total score and use the interpretive table that follows the survey to understand your team's situation and how you might apply a network-centred leadership approach to your team's work.

Survey questions
Does each team member understand the external environment?
Are the team's goals clear and stable?
Is the work of the team, and are the methods to be used, clear and agreed?
Are the interfaces between this team and others clear and effective?
Do the people in the team 'speak the same language'?
Does the team have valuable solutions for each market and opportunity?
Does the team have the capabilities that it needs to achieve its goals?
Are people in the team actively engaged on the key priorities?
Is the team using social platforms successfully?
Is the team consistently learning and improving its productivity?
Does the team have a single dashboard that is clear, effective and shared?
Do team members have time to stop and think?

No This is seldom the case					Yes This is usually the case
0	1	2	3	4	5
0	1	2	3	4	5
0	1	2	3	4	5
0	1	2	3	4	5
0	1	2	3	4	5
0	1	2	3	4	5
0	1	2	3	4	5
0	1	2	3	4	5
0	1	2	3	4	5
0	1	2	3	4	5
0	1	2	3	4	5
0	1	2	3	4	5

Total (highest possible score = 60) _____

Understanding your team's situation

Score	Description of the environment	Consider using network-centred leadership to:
0–12	There is no common understanding of the current situation, and no common language or approach. No design for the future state exists. Often strategy is described in PowerPoint decks with little or no contextual narrative. Progress, when it happens, is due to the heroic actions of a few people. Leaders may feel highly empowered.	**Define** the new environment
13–24	People have started talking about the real issues. A future state, an operating approach and specific measures are being designed and agreed. Basic disciplines and rules of thumb are emerging. Unconnected measures of progress are in use.	**Design** new solutions and methods
25–36	An agreed approach is being pursued by unconnected groups across the organisation. Clear value propositions are available but may not be consistently executed. Leaders have, or are developing, the capabilities they need.	**Develop** critical new capabilities
37–48	The people in the organisation have reliable operating models and propositions and the ability to change these models to match changing circumstances. The right people seem to be in each of the critical roles. Constructive dialogue, based on a common language, occurs between groups.	**Deliver** consistently

Score	Description of the environment	Consider using network-centred leadership to:
49–60	Things just work. Structural and cultural issues have been resolved and the new approach delivers the anticipated commercial results. Irritation dissipates and leaders are rewarded. If the context starts to evolve, changes are recognised early and the necessary adjustments to people, approaches and tools are made.	**Observe** the environment for potential risk

Building capability

You can repeat this survey across groups and over time to measure the leadership quality and progress of an individual, team or organisation. Team leaders typically score teams more favourably than team members.

Network-centred leadership typically develops in stages. Imagine the work of leadership as a ladder of increasing capability (Figure 33).[99] It shows how a group with unintegrated, ad hoc ideas can become a capable team delivering value, despite ongoing change.

Each step on the ladder builds on the success of the previous steps. Assuming that each step is being executed with good judgement, the organisational or team capability should improve in a predictable fashion. Logically, if an organisation or team has a shared context, a good plan and capable people, then it should achieve strong upward momentum.

Figure 33. A capability ladder

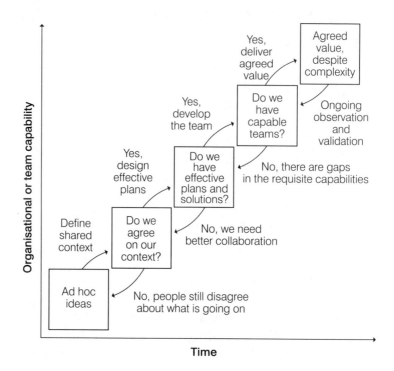

Getting started

To start using network-centred leadership, we recommend that you list the challenges that you are currently working on. As you read Part 3, start applying the approach to a couple of your challenges to see how network-centred leadership can work for you.

The final four chapters of the book are designed to support the implementation of network-centred leadership in your organisation or team. They build on the ideas presented in Parts 1 and 2. We have repeated some of the material so that you can use each chapter in Part 3 independently as a reference.

Part 3

Executing network-centred leadership

Chapter 10
Defining your context

'The single biggest problem in communication is the
illusion that it has taken place.'
- George Bernard Shaw -

Major programs and strategies are inherently abstract and
complicated. There are usually as many views as there are people
involved. Leaders cannot assume that the members of a team are
clear about, or able to describe, their context or plans.

This chapter describes how to use a network map to create a
shared picture of context. Making a small investment to ensure
that people are 'on the same page' helps to develop a shared
understanding of a team's current position and provide a sound
basis for team leadership.

A definition of context

Context refers to the set of circumstances or facts that surround
a particular team, strategy or program of work. It includes the
current vision and goals of a team or organisation, language, mental
models, specific historical agreements, goals and descriptions of
the environment. Ideally, all the people engaged with a particular
piece of work will understand:

- the history of the organisation, its markets, products
  and services

- the organisation's strategic choices, structure and major 'chunks' of work, which are in place as a result of historical decisions

- the place of a leader and/or team's work in the broader work of the organisation ('this team is building X, or delivering Y')

- the governance arrangements around the leader and/or team

- the relevant goals, targets and key performance indicators for the leader and/or team

- the composition of the team currently engaged in the work

- the team's key operations and their inputs and outputs

- the sources of feedback that are being monitored, internally and externally

- the current improvement initiatives in progress

- the process for accessing training materials to address key skills gaps.

Planning, by contrast, describes the various strategies, plans and tactics that may be implemented to achieve the goals.

The difference between context and a plan is akin to the difference between a balance sheet and an income statement. The context describes the state of the team or organisation at a point in time, like a balance sheet. Plans, and planning, address the things that should occur looking forward. Each year, old plans are executed and new plans are created. The context evolves. Asking for the current context is like asking for the current balance sheet.

The need for shared context

Context is important because communication is only effective when the parties involved have enough common language and experience to understand each other. It may be a financial deal conducted in Mandarin, or a construction dispute in an English court, but words need to have broadly the same meaning for the participants. When miscommunications occur, enough common ground is needed to address the error.[100]

In a traditional environment, this shared context is provided by the hierarchical leader. A leader makes a plan and shares it with his or her team members, who in turn make subsidiary plans with their teams. Each part can be described as the leader sees fit. When gaps emerge between people, or where gaps exist between the plan and the reality, the leader can resolve the difference.

Traditional planning methods, which involve setting budgets and allocating resources on an annual basis, can be used to support this hierarchy and provide coordination across the various parts of the plan and organisation.

The impact of complexity

The challenge facing senior leadership is to make sure that teams have a similar shared language and understanding of context in complex environments. Experience suggests that this is seldom the case. Most people involved in strategy are using individual mental models, not shared frameworks. Often, diverse teams have little in common.[101] Jargon overtakes language and, before too long, people are afraid to say that they don't know what is going on for fear of looking silly. People aren't on the same page.

When the environment is dynamic, these issues are compounded. As the speed of change accelerates, leaders cannot process all the changes fast enough to keep up. In addition, leaders may not know enough in the new environment to devise an appropriate plan or resolve an issue intelligently. Communication breaks down when differences in language occur. Decision rights become unclear and unfiltered information flows accelerate the confusion.

Some leaders respond by hoping that each team will organically create a useful plan or model of their context that will address this problem. Theory and experience suggest that this is uncommon. It is much more likely that participants will come to a grudging accommodation, after considerable cost and delay.

An explicit framework is required

If leaders cannot assume that people understand what is required, or hope that they will pick it up through 'osmosis', then the team needs to actively create and manage an explicit description. Having a clear understanding of context provides a coherent foundation for the team, as they try to respond to change by integrating different perspectives and resetting direction.

A suitable framework may simply be a set of documents that the leader and team agree represents the 'single version of the truth' for the team. Rather than having hundreds of disconnected presentations, spreadsheets and emails, a team may only have a few agreed documents and systems that fit together into a single coherent picture. These can be discussed and refined using a common language. Roles and responsibilities are allocated based on these documents and systems. As the environment, work or teams change, the documents and systems are updated to ensure alignment. That way, all the team members have access to the latest information.

Even in traditional environments, investing to clarify context in this way may be valuable. It facilitates knowledge transfer and reduces the risk of losing capability, especially in the event of generational change.

Work as a method to clarify context

Building a common understanding is now a major challenge. In many ways, it has become harder to clarify success than to achieve it. Even with capable people, it can take weeks or months to get a team to express and resolve the different points of view about what is going on.

Focusing on work provides a way to clarify context. The question, 'What work do you need to do to execute your program or strategy?' provides a useful starting point for a conversation that will identify the various work streams. This question typically produces a list of all the productive, or operative, activities in an organisation, or across organisations. After talking about work with different people in a group, a jigsaw puzzle of overlapping ideas and activities typically emerges. These can apply at different levels of abstraction (that is, at different 'altitudes') in the organisation.

A leader can:

- sort the various issues and the work into piles or 'chunks' that are relatively autonomous. The objective is to allow a team of people to work on each chunk in a comparatively stand-alone fashion.[102] Some chunks will need traditional leadership approaches while others will be collaborative.

- model each chunk of work as a hub in a network. Interactions between chunks of work can be displayed as interfaces between hubs in the network.

- represent the connected hubs as a map (Figure 34).

Figure 34. Work as a network map of connected hubs

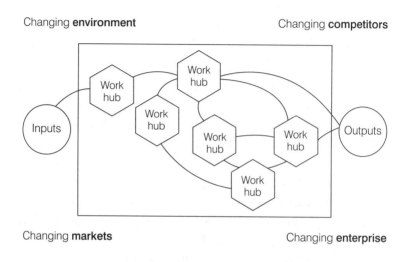

This approach produces a surprisingly clear and robust picture, even in complex environments. If drawn at the right altitude, it can provide a stable framework for leadership, combining a mix of hierarchical, project and collaborative approaches.[103] The mix between the three approaches can vary by issue, and over time, because the work has been separated by clear interfaces.[104]

Individuals can contribute to some hubs, but not others, as required. This is not an attempt to restrict communication, but is rather a way to maintain attention and concentrate effort on the key priorities, reducing the risk of cognitive overload. Framing the work as hubs makes it easier to clarify information flows and decision making, both of which are critical to successful execution.[105]

As important as the map itself, the process of discussing and sorting these various descriptions of work into a unified model is an important step towards creating an effective team. As the process is applied across a team, it helps various team members to appreciate the various perspectives and responsibilities of those around them. It also creates a single common language to discuss work and priorities.

One of Waypoint's clients describes his adoption of transparency in this way:

> When I first became CEO, it was as if all my knowledge was contained in 100 boxes. No-one, not even my wife or my trusted professional adviser, knew the contents of all the boxes. I shared my thinking as I thought necessary. Of course, I was always disappointed that my team failed to grasp the critical nuances of our situation as quickly or as keenly as I did. It took me some time, including a stint as a non-executive director on another board, to realise the value of transparency and to understand that the critical factor was not what was in each box but how my team and I could take that collective knowledge, add to it and come up with a better solution.

Networks as a method to execute strategy

In most organisations, the formulation of strategy and major program execution are processes that require consistent, integrated activity over a period of years. Each leader's approach to their work evolves to reflect the growing capability of the team, the changing business environment, and the status of the plan.

All the evolving ideas and work are intertwined. Leaders need to share ideas, ask questions and express their knowledge so that they can align their critical work with the changing needs of the other parts of the organisation. The rise of matrix organisations, partnerships and virtual teams reflects and compounds this communication challenge.

Organising the work as a network and using a more distributed leadership approach is far more stable than traditional methods, particularly in complex environments. As discussed, role-based hierarchies break down, often in predictable ways.

Networks and hubs provide more flexibility. They should be able to adapt to their changing environment if a few simple guidelines and governance limits are followed. At each hub, teams can choose to pursue their goals in a variety of ways and adapt without impacting other hubs. Leaders can also adjust using simple decision rules. Intel's 'maximise wafer profitability' rule (discussed in Chapter 4) is an example of this kind of approach.

In one example, a leader managing the Asian region for a multinational company inherited a planning approach that set revenue and cost goals for each country from the regional office. As the countries' economies fluctuated, this approach broke down because country managers needed to adapt to the changing environment. To address this, the leader moved to a principle-based approach. He challenged leaders to grow sales faster than GDP by a fixed percentage and to increase costs at a rate less than GDP growth. This freed local leaders from an ongoing negotiation with the regional office and allowed them to focus on their markets.

A general summary of the higher level program (documenting key terms and ideas, values and assumptions) can then be applied across the network to set a foundation for relationships between hubs, and across the broader organisation.

Creating this kind of model may require a significant investment and a change in leader behaviour. However, it can provide matching benefits. Case Study 11 provides another example of the power of establishing an agreed, unified context as a basis for realigning work.

Case Study 11
Realigning a program to materially improve outcomes

A leader running a major defence program engaged us following a critical external review and contract renegotiation. He was thinking about how best to meet the various new demands of his different stakeholders, delivery and cost performance targets, innovation goals, and contract compliance requirements. Different stakeholders and team members had varying levels of understanding about the new expectations. To be successful, the program leader knew that he needed to get everybody 'on the same page'.

We facilitated a conversation with the program team that focused on the various definitions of success and the work streams that were implied by each definition. Once the goals and work had been untangled, a clear and shared picture of the program emerged. This showed the program to be at the intersection of two higher order networks: a government organisation and the military on the one hand (together the 'enterprise' shown horizontally in Figure 35) and the goals of the company (reflecting shareholder intent).

The team built a hub around this detailed picture to align the various work streams according to a common scoreboard. This provided a shared context. The team also worked with the broader company and the enterprise to ensure a common understanding of the new environment. Critical information was clarified and feedback loops established. With a coherent description of their context in place, the team has gone on to exceed industry-wide service benchmarks and deliver superior program outcomes.

Figure 35. The broader context of a defence program

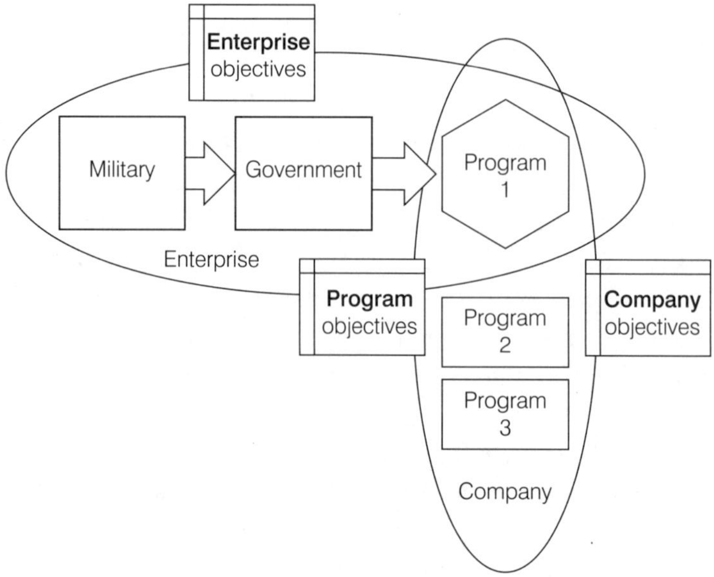

Describing the work of a team at a hub

Each hub on a network map represents a 'chunk' of work, or work stream, which typically requires a team of up to 150 people.[106] Groups of this size can function effectively, but if teams contain more than 150 people, they are likely to subdivide.

Hubs can be used to support stand-alone projects, or can be linked internally or externally to reflect natural work groups and business needs. This might be across the various parts of a supply chain, a contract or an external process. Once the work has been clarified and sorted, it is usually much easier to describe the context at each hub.

A simple way to get started is to label the large hexagon provided in Figure 36. The labels should include:

- an overall description of the hub

- key inputs, outputs, interfaces and elements of governance

- forces affecting the size and shape of your environment

- key chunks of work that you are doing or need to do.

Figure 36. Outline of a network hub

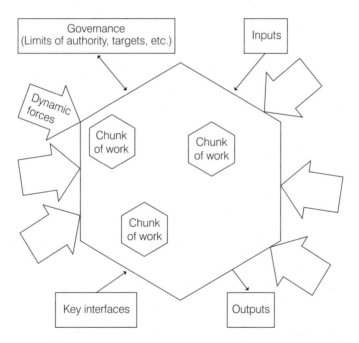

Clarifying 'non-negotiables'

It is important to clarify what must be maintained across the hub. Typically, there are three kinds of 'non-negotiables' that meet this description:

- the key measures, or broader mission, that frame success

- the key behaviours that are expected of everybody who works at the hub

- the key executional considerations that apply at the hub. These may range from such things as meeting debt covenants, to stipulating opening hours and defining key deliverables.

A dynamic systems lens

The work at any hub can be modelled as a dynamic system, as opposed to a static process (Figure 37).

Figure 37. Model of work as a dynamic control system

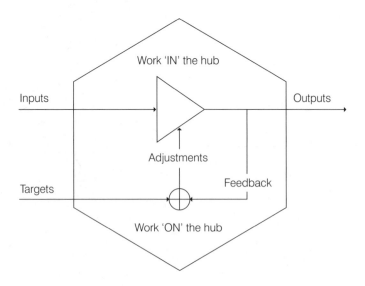

Each team will typically perform some basic operation, turning inputs into outputs (this can be called the work *in* a hub). In addition, the team will be monitoring feedback from various sources to adjust their operations to better meet a range of targets (the work *on* a hub).

While the work can be separated into two types, both are usually done by the same team of people. The mix of work in a hub will help to determine the appropriate organisational structure and leadership approach.

If most of the work is being processed *in* the hub, it will typically require traditional leadership methods, such as process control. The social platform information factory model described in Chapter 3 works well in this environment.

As the rate of change and the complexity of the work increases, the work *on* the hub becomes more important. Project approaches become more critical and valuable. In these cases, the information factory breaks down and online campuses become more appropriate.

Key interfaces

Once a hub has been created, leaders should consider four factors that influence the key interfaces with other hubs and within the hub itself: key relationships, team governance, supporting networks, and the hub's direction and rate of change.

Key relationships

Management of relationships is obviously critical to any organisation. In networks, these are represented as interfaces between hubs. The most successful adaptive systems balance the number of interfaces that connect them to other parts of the network.[107] If too few interfaces are taken seriously, a team will not get the signals that it needs to change. If too many interfaces are incorporated, the team will become disoriented and unstable as people try to serve too many masters.

Once the number of key relationships has been agreed, the work to manage each relationship needs to be undertaken.

Team governance

The most important interface is the one that points upwards. Often, this is a relationship with the next layer of management, but increasingly it involves dealing with a more complex governance environment, like a board. There is a lot that can be written about governance, particularly board governance.[108] In its simplest form, governance is simply the framework and intent that is provided to a team from the next layer of management. This may be via specific targets, limits of authority, or suggestions, either formal or informal.

To create an effective work environment, governance discussion needs to establish context for the hub, specifically the:

• vision, mission and purpose of the group

• acceptable values and behaviours

• work environment (shared language, organisation, meeting and communication protocols)

• overall business model or framework to create value

• limits (or delegations) of authority.

This context sets a foundation for work, behaviours and communications and exposes the scope available to each team. This construct can create an environment in which participants can derive meaning, a feeling of belonging and a sense of worth. These factors are important for performance.[109]

Supporting networks

More generally, work can have different levels of abstraction, or what we call 'altitude'.[110] Some work may take more time, have larger or more sophisticated outputs, or require more abstract methods.[111] This can be visualised as a series of network maps at different levels, shown previously in Figure 19.

Each hub receives its governance from the layer above and support from the network of hubs at lower levels of altitude. Put another way, the hubs at one level can be decomposed into entire networks at the lower level, with each hub creating context for the layer below.

The hub's direction and rate of change

Leaders will typically want to give teams a sense of where the work has come from and where it is going. Hubs develop in predictable ways. Teams typically do one of three things to improve performance:[112]

- **'get fit' and 'stay fit'** work to improve the current function of the hub, i.e. drive financial performance and commercial discipline

- **'change the rules'** work to change the function of the hub, i.e. accelerate ways to exploit current industry 'givens' such as changing the industry value chain or moving the focus to adjacent markets.

- **'change the game'** by working to alter the network and repositioning, deleting or merging the hub, i.e. identify opportunities to transform the company, radically change the business model or undertake a transition to new markets.

The strategy to improve a hub's performance can be represented as a ladder of increasing value (Figure 38).

Figure 38. Strategies to improve performance in a hub

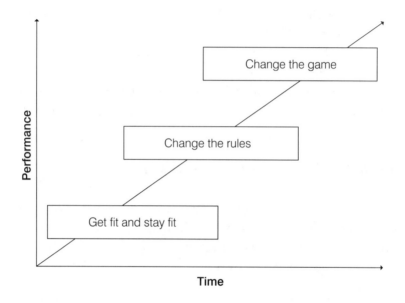

Chapter 11
Designing effective plans and solutions

'The explanation requiring the fewest assumptions is
most likely to be correct.'
~ William of Ockham ~

Network-centred leadership provides a way to navigate change by
focusing on written collaboration around the work at each hub
in a network.[113] By using the same approach to clarify each piece
of work, leaders can build a work culture that will stand up to
the rigours of complexity and ensure that assumptions are being
exposed, real collaboration is occurring, and the best possible
portfolio of options and solutions is being developed.

Making a plan for a hub

In a traditional environment, expertise about markets, products
and operations allows leaders to make informed annual forecasts.
Companies have a range of effective planning techniques.

Network-centred leadership asks teams to invest the necessary
time during these processes to ensure that these plans are robust
enough to cope with the emergence of complexity. At a minimum,
the leader and team at each hub should discuss the context and
write out a draft of the work that needs to be done to achieve their
goals. This will expose their thoughts and questions to each other

and can lead to a safe conversation. Team members can help to close gaps in logic, expertise or skill, as appropriate.

If the challenge turns out to be straightforward, network-centred leadership can be as simple as a leader writing a problem statement, making a task list and discussing it with their team. If the team feels safe and is willing to discuss the problem statement and task list, assumptions can be confirmed and improvements integrated. Capability gaps can be addressed with training. At this point, a leader and team can 'declare victory' and pick another problem, or opportunity, to work on. Completing a number of small projects builds momentum and confidence in the approach and the leader.

Provided leaders have the required political and technical skills to incorporate these skills into the team, the approach will also be successful in other environments where customer, political or technical uncertainties exist.

Even when the problem is complex, a leader will be successful if the team members feel comfortable with a collaborative approach. The team will identify the problem as complex and cycle through the four Ds of network-centred leadership: define, design, develop and deliver. Somebody will propose a draft of the appropriate work. Others will disagree, contributing and building on the approach until a credible trial has been created. They will, for instance, be able to identify root causes, or the interests of a market. The proposed trial will be conducted and evaluated. Implied tasks will be identified and addressed. Once proven, resources can be added to expand the successful approach.

This kind of collaboration helps leaders to design the optimal approach, balance positive initiatives and controls, and mitigate the political risk if a trial proves unsuccessful. Collaborative cultures can run lots of these kinds of trials to find a way forward without anybody losing face, or their reputation.

Making a plan for a network

Leaders are typically looking simultaneously to create new business models that suit the dynamic environment, and to operate their current businesses. They typically need to use collaborative approaches to find new revenue streams and hierarchical leadership approaches to efficiently drive the current business model.

Finding ways to build new revenue streams and business models is a subject well canvased by analysts in the fields of design, marketing, innovation and product development. A number of authors and researchers have made the link between the successful methods of software development and broader project and management planning.[114] A detailed discussion of these various techniques is outside the scope of this book.

In addition, leaders may need to develop multiple options and scenarios to suit changing circumstances. Various analogies have been used to describe this approach: planning alternative flight paths, building a play book (as in sports), or playing a hand of cards.

Regardless of how you think about it, a leader needs to be able to apply different leadership approaches to the various work streams and choose between various options in real time without suffering cognitive overload. This is too much to expect from a single leader. Leaders and teams will inevitably need to collaborate. There are a few reasons for this:

- New ideas often come from capable people who have diverse points of view.

- Execution typically requires the cooperation of many people.

- Options that don't work may create political risk.

- Organisational functions need information and time to adjust if they are to support new offers and approaches.

- Different options have different financial consequences, which need to be included in any assessment.

- Job descriptions typically don't keep up with the changing needs of the team, so the HR people need to be included.

A network map provides a basis for this collaboration. It allows teams to break the situation up into components, each with an appropriate leadership approach. The forces that were defined in the previous chapter can help to prepare the team for the dynamic environment. Teams can review each of the various forces that shape the team, or their organisation. They can ask, 'What would happen if each in turn was increased, or decreased, by an order of magnitude?' Various combinations of change can be grouped together to create a range of scenarios.

Planning to accommodate these various scenarios usually requires the development of a traditional base plan supported by various initiatives that a leader might make, depending on the circumstances. Initiatives may be of various types, including:

- investments that an organisation might make

- deals that might be won

- movement of key individuals

- selection of methods for particular processes

- messages that might be sent to key partners and/or stakeholders.

By framing these as a set of discrete options, they can sit alongside the traditional planning process, to be used when appropriate. Case Study 12 provides an example of how Waypoint helped a client close its performance gap by explicitly mapping and evaluating incremental options.

Case Study 12

Closing the performance gap by mapping and evaluating options

One of our clients ran a services company hit by an economic downturn. Unable to meet his budget through traditional operations, the CEO wanted to develop a series of potential incremental options (involving both transactions and joint ventures) that could close the budget gap. Each option had different benefits and risk profiles. In addition, there was a level of interconnectedness between the alternatives.

He engaged us to help his team develop various options to meet the budget. We worked with the team to clarify the various options and create a single execution plan that would close the budget gap. A diagram similar to Figure 39 was used to frame the various options.

The agreed options and discussion helped the team to decide what to do in real time. As circumstances evolved, the team successfully executed a number of the options and achieved their target.

Figure 39. Closing the performance gap with incremental profit options

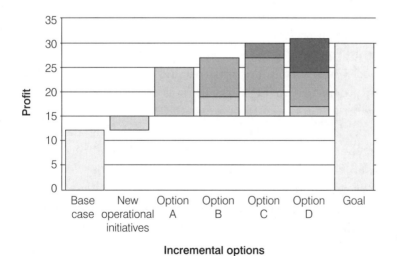

Incremental options

The risks and benefits of structured discussion

Discussing the timing, sequencing and nature of various strategy options can be challenging for teams. Most people are naturally curious and have a personal stake in some options more than others. In the past, leaders could keep the commercially and politically sensitive discussions private, but increasingly this is impossible because of the transparency afforded by modern communication technologies.

Getting the right people involved in any piece of work remains critical. Striking the balance between confidentiality and capability is more challenging because more people need to be involved if the team is to build a complete picture and have the requisite capabilities. Inevitably, managing these conversations depends on the character and maturity of the team.

Once the composition of a team is set, there is likely to be a vigorous conversation in which positions and views are sorted out and organised. Such conversations are inevitable. The challenge is to facilitate them in a way that builds shared understanding, as quickly and effectively as possible.[115] As people start working together and dealing with issues, facilitated discussion can help to ensure that early miscommunications are addressed and a safe environment is created.

This conversation has significant additional benefits. How leaders contribute to an initiative and develop new capabilities greatly depends on how the work is framed.[116] Adults have a range of accumulated knowledge and experience, which can be represented by different mental models. Asking questions in different ways, and in different formats, can produce a variety of answers that improve performance and help in the development of new capabilities.

Humans are good at watching each other and learning what to do in a given situation by referring to others for cues.[117] Overhearing the discussions of your peers, and the kinds of issues and questions they are dealing with, will lead to richer communication and an earlier recognition of issues. Online systems can support this process by allowing visibility between leaders about the work each is doing.

Finally, a focus on specific work, rather than roles, depersonalises conversations and reduces personal resistance when changes need to be made. If, for example, a work delay occurs, documents can be referenced and modified without it being seen as a personal criticism of a team member.

Network maps as a basis for safe collaboration

Network maps can help with the challenge of safe collaboration because they naturally involve organising people into smaller groups that address more manageable problems.

Creating social cohesion and alignment across an organisation is hard. It is much easier to achieve it in smaller teams.[118] With a network map, teams only have to worry about their particular hub. They have a shared basis for planning and collaboration.

While meetings can be helpful when establishing a team and starting a discussion, it is also helpful if the leader and/or the team write a description of the problem, or opportunity, and describe what they consider to be the best way forward. This written model may be in a range of forms (decision trees, documents, spreadsheets, etc.). Initially, it may be no more than a problem statement or a list of alternative ideas. But as the discussion matures, it can develop into a proper range of options and initiatives. In other words, a plan will emerge.

If a team cannot write a plan down in some form, it tells leaders that the environment may not be safe, or that the leader and team are not yet sufficiently capable of proceeding, and that further development is required. But the issues will have been identified at an early stage and the necessary adjustments can be made.

When a team takes time to create a written model, it helps with the quality of both the plan and the social collaboration in a number of ways. A written model:

1. takes the plan out of the leader's head and exposes the proposed approach and alternative scenarios to team and peer review. This exposes assumptions for discussion, gives permission for people to ask questions and provide feedback, and grounds everybody in the specific work to be done.

2. creates a shared language and provides a basis for discussions about roles, decision rights and information flows.[119] If anybody has ideas or problems, they can discuss them more easily by using the model as a reference.

3. addresses some of the social issues within teams by providing shared context

4. encourages conversations that can sometimes be missing, or delayed, in a traditional environment. At this time, uncommitted or inadequately trained leaders can be identified, support can be provided and plans can be refined or redeveloped.

5. builds accountability by specifically assigning work to individual leaders. Mismatched rewards and penalties for success and failure can be exposed as leaders review the various roles they are expected to perform.

Handling issues of psychological safety

As discussions progress, it is not unusual for some team members to disengage or react negatively. Some people cannot, or will not, participate in a collaborative process of any kind. The psychological risks may be too great. Or there may be a whole other range of issues in play.

In these cases, leaders should start by taking the issue away from the team so that a private conversation can be had in which the individual's specific issues are addressed.

More generally, organisations can manage collaboration in a number of ways. Everybody has more than enough to do. They don't need to be involved with the development of every piece of work. It may be better to have a smaller team of 'volunteers' than a larger army of 'conscripts'.

In organisations where most leadership work is traditional, there is little need for leaders to modify their style. They can simply let others solve the small set of problems that require collaboration. If most of the leadership work across an organisation requires ongoing collaboration, individuals may still be able to retreat to a specialist position. However, if they want to remain engaged with leadership work, they have no choice but to find collaborative approaches where they can be successful.

Leaders who are not prepared to discuss important issues are increasingly likely to be bypassed by a community using a social platform to avoid the traditional hierarchy. The next generation of employees is comfortable with collaborative tools and approaches, and is simply unprepared to wait for a leader who is using what they see as a secretive or obsolete approach.

Teaching as a measure of plan quality

Once a team has a clear context and plan, teaching is a great way to confirm the plan's quality. Aristotle wrote that 'the proof that you know something is that you are able to teach it'. This remains a valid test today.

Leaders who regularly teach their context, base plan and options to relevant audiences will confirm their understanding, ensure the adequacy of their plans and improve their teams on an ongoing basis. They can clarify their own thoughts, receive feedback and confirm the state of their teams.

Encouraging leaders to explain their work makes it explicit and clarifies their mental models. This can feel cumbersome, slow and uncomfortable for the leader involved, but it provides a language and level of self-awareness that is critical for productive collaboration, mental flexibility and development. If leaders are more aware of their context and options, they are more likely to select the right mental model and develop the required skills.

The act of creating teaching materials helps leaders to develop. Most corporate training involves static information, which gives leaders little opportunity to practise the activities they are reading about. Alternatively, training is delivered as case studies, which are hard to translate into the client's environment. Writing a speech, or constructing online resources about the real problems that the team faces, is a terrific development experience for leaders. When they are expressing and presenting methods, goals or leadership options for others to see, their personal stake in what is happening is a lot higher. A lot of self-checking and reflection takes place, which increases development.

Teams also benefit from this process. Being explicit with larger groups forces team members to be clear about the full portfolio of initiatives in progress. It helps to deliver a set of goals (the breadth of the work) and the specific activities and work progress required to deliver each outcome (the depth of the work). When it comes to executing the options, the team is prepared.

Effective knowledge management can improve performance

Leaders who face new situations often want to reapply something that has worked before, especially when strong research supports that approach. When knowledge transfer of this kind is possible, it has the potential to significantly improve innovation, productivity and performance.

Most organisations use reports, job descriptions, training materials and processes[120] as the basis for knowledge management.

These work well within a particular context, provided leaders can maintain both the structure and content of the material. People simply take the last version of a report and change the relevant details.

While these methods work well when work is being repeated, they are less effective for packaging strategic options between teams or situations. There are a number of reasons for this:

- Previously used processes may not be valuable when applied in a different situation or context. Information cannot be reapplied directly for any issue more complex than a simple process.[121] A 'cookie cutter' approach often fails because each situation and context is different. To be useful for major programs, information must be packaged at the right altitude. It must have the right level of abstraction, so that it can be successfully reapplied to a different context with different team members and in a different environment.

- Training materials, while relevant, are typically not specific enough to provide meaningful direction for leaders acting in real time. The cognitive effort to apply the training to the specific situation is nearly as great as designing a solution from first principles.

- It is hard to clarify what information is important and how it may be reapplied. People have very different ideas about what is important and why it is useful. In addition, these views can change over time, as circumstances change.

- Information can be sorted and described in a wide variety of ways. Increasingly, people use different terms and languages to describe similar ideas. Creating a common social context becomes an important part of any successful capture and reapplication of information.[122]

- Social capital and networks of understanding that exist in one context, and which make a particular approach successful, often don't transfer. The materials need to be rebuilt in the new context.[123]

- Practically, the only way to manage this much information is through an online repository where it can be searched, tagged and hyperlinked. That way, the information is closely linked to the system that is used to house it.

Case Study 13 shows how we have overcome these issues and created a knowledge base that can be valuably applied in different situations.

Case Study 13
Using knowledge to improve consulting performance

Both authors keep a wide range of books, articles and documents. Over time, we have amassed a library of thousands of items. In addition, good-quality research and references are available on every aspect of business via the internet. We have sorted and re-sorted this information over time, looking for a way to make sense of this mass of material.

Over the past five years, we have tried various methods to ensure that our library is more than just another knowledge 'graveyard'. We needed to find a way of packaging information that allowed the information to be effectively reapplied. We tried various options to create, capture, maintain and use information.

We have now recognised that it is not possible to reapply content directly to different situations. General solutions don't work because each organisation is a unique network of work hubs, operating in its own context. However, we have found that most organisational networks are made up of a collection of 10 different kinds of hubs (Figure 40). Within each of these general hubs, there are a number of relevant tools, approaches and frameworks that can be applied with judgement.

We are now focused on building patterns that can support our judgement as consultants when we are working at one of these hubs. The focus of our research has moved from selecting particular techniques to matching tools to various situations and describing success factors and risks.

Figure 40. Generic executive work hubs

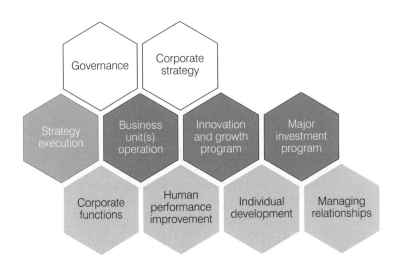

Patterns provide a way to transfer knowledge between hubs

Patterns are a way to capture and reapply knowledge to support human judgement. They have been successfully used in a number of fields, from architecture to software development.[124] Patterns provide an outline of the work at a new hub. They are a place to start a conversation, not a replacement for judgement.

A pattern is a package of information that helps leaders to solve a critical problem that occurs repeatedly in an organisation.[125]

It is not used to provide a 'cookie cutter' solution. Instead, it characterises the problems that are to be solved, the context or situations where these problems arise, and the conditions under which the proposed solutions can be recommended. Often these problems arise from a conflict of interests or forces. A pattern emerges as a dialogue, which helps to work out how to balance the forces and finally make a decision.

Patterns will vary, and they evolve based on the needs of each organisation. They will work at different levels of altitude and have different levels of maturity, depending on how well the people in the organisation explicitly understand their work. In a business context, the kinds of information that are helpful include:

- descriptions of the work

- glossaries of key terms

- scoreboards and benchmarks

- key mental models and frameworks to assist with analysis

- lists of options with assessments of pros and cons

- forms and templates

- lessons learned

- key references.

The challenge when creating a pattern is to identify and document the key ideas that make it easy to distinguish a good solution from a poor solution. The next step is to provide information that will assist in the design of future solutions. The ideas expressed in a pattern should be general enough to be applied in very different situations, but they must still be specific enough to give constructive guidance.

It is easy to assume that typical problems have a limited set of solutions and leaders must choose either one or another of a fixed set of solutions. Good patterns encourage solutions that overcome the inherent limits of this thinking.[126]

Patterns develop over time. One can think about the process as the distillation of information into knowledge. Initially, a new business situation is a mystery that people need to explore and understand through experimentation. As lessons are learned about the new environment, models are formed that allow people to predict cause and effect. Finally, algorithms are created to automate and optimise the required trade-offs.[127]

Case Study 14 demonstrates how an investment in knowledge has improved our own service delivery.

Case Study 14
How patterns help leaders navigate role transition

Our focus on work and capability means that we are regularly asked to help people make a transition to a new role in a new company.

Over the past 14 years, we have helped over 600 people with transition. For the first 500 clients (before our investments in LEEP), we treated each individual in a bespoke manner, spending a number of hours working through their personal situations. Over the past few years, however, we have built everything we know about this process into two patterns: 'career transition' and 'the first 100 days'. In each, we have assembled what we believe to be a useful collection of reference material to help leaders who are looking for, or starting, their role. This includes proven activities, references, planning templates and risk management approaches.

Each time we wish to help somebody, we start by copying and personalising one of the patterns. We then give the client appropriate access to the material on a hub. As we take each new person through the two patterns, we inevitably see things in a new light and learn about new aspects of the process. These insights help us improve the patterns for future use.

The productivity of our service delivery has improved significantly as a result of this change, and with no loss of quality. We now only spend an hour or so with each leader, down from three to five hours in the bespoke approach. Moreover, we have an online real-time method of engaging with those individuals who want to maintain a dialogue or use us as a sounding board.

A number of clients have customised our 'first 100 days' pattern to create a bespoke approach that works for them. They now copy, distribute and improve their bespoke pattern as part of their more specific orientation efforts.

Knowledge management is only valuable in certain circumstances

Knowledge management is difficult, and should not be undertaken lightly. Creating and managing useful patterns can be expensive and time consuming.[128] This kind of investment can only be justified when reapplication is likely to produce a material improvement in productivity. This is typically when problems are repeated across an organisation.

To date, five areas have been identified where investments in knowledge management can significantly improve executive performance:

1. **Orientation**—Helping people who join a team to understand the context and have an appropriate level of key skills is more easily achieved if the context of the program is outlined in writing. Typically, this outline will contain:

   • the context, as described in the previous chapter (values, approach)

- general skills and reminders associated with joining a new program

- training for critical tools, systems or methods.

2. **Service delivery**—Simple services can be managed as processes, but when they become more sophisticated and dynamic, they need to be supported differently.[129] The introduction of customisation can create significant variations between the best, and worst, client service. To address this, leaders typically benefit from:

- detailed descriptions of the value propositions and case studies

- process training for the relevant systems that the team uses.

3. **Critical roles**—These include cohorts of leaders such as a store manager, country manager or contract manager. In each case, multiple people are performing a similar role. The organisation is sensitive to the performance of the leaders in these roles and there is significant variation between the best and worst performer.

4. **Decision pipelines**—These can help manage critical resource allocations, such as a list of initiatives awaiting capital approval, or a list of new products being developed. In each case, there is likely to be relevant knowledge about the overall process, the format of applications, decision criteria, and a live history of the decisions that have been made, or are to be made in the future.

5. **Key interfaces**—This may be the flow of information to the board, contract management with a key customer or

supplier, or key internal interfaces. In each case, there is likely to be agreed standards of performance, methods for communication, key documents that define the interface, and a live history of the decisions that have been made in relation to the interface. A good example of a key interface is the relationship between a board and management.

If managed correctly, patterns can become a significant source of competitive advantage over time.[130] They can be at least part of the valuable digital capabilities that successful companies are using to compete in new markets.

Chapter 12
Developing capable teams

'Before you become too entranced with gorgeous gadgets and
mesmerizing video displays, let me remind you that information
is not knowledge, knowledge is not wisdom, and wisdom is not
foresight. Each grows out of the other, and we need them all.'
~ Arthur C. Clarke ~

The choices that each organisation makes about leadership,
organisational structure and supporting human resource systems
are likely to have a major effect on competitive performance.
Successful organisations will be those that find 'sweet spots'
aligned with dynamic markets.

To be capable, individuals, teams and organisations need to be
able to execute the changing portfolio of work described by the
network map. People will need to adjust to the changing needs of
the work, learn quickly, take various positions in a team and use
alternative approaches as required.

This chapter addresses four questions that companies need
to answer if they are to develop capable leaders, teams and
organisations. It explains how the network framework and focus
on work can help organisations make better decisions about
leadership design, selection and development.

How should organisations be designed?

Historically, the senior management team has decided the strategy and structure for a company through a top-down process. They work with line leaders and the HR team to cascade the strategy through the organisation and build capable teams to execute the strategy.

When senior leaders are successful, the organisation is tightly aligned with the strategy and market positioning. As work is done, value flows to customers, owners and employees.

However, as markets have become more dynamic and competitive, product life cycles have shortened dramatically. Successful enterprise-wide value propositions are in short supply. Many companies need a portfolio of offers supported by different business models and organisations. They must continually reinvest to maintain their competitive position. This requires far more leadership effort and has a profound effect on the size and shape of organisations.

To frame the discussion, consider two types of organisations: a hierarchy using traditional approaches, and a dynamic organisation with a flat structure and effective collaborative techniques. These structures may exist within an entity, or across a distributed social network.

Organisations will increasingly need a mix of both models to support different types of work and businesses. Even in the most traditional organisations, social platforms will be used to empower the informal organisation, creating a collaborative network that crosses divisional boundaries and, in many cases, short-circuits formal processes. Even the most dynamic firms have supporting hierarchies that include cohorts, and that stipulate staff functions to some degree. In both environments, leaders will naturally use project teams for issues such as the integration of an acquisition, the start-up of a joint venture project, or the launch of a new business initiative.

The best answer for any company will depend on its context, the level of complexity it faces, and the strategy it is pursuing. If, as we contend, work is becoming more complex, it means that leadership needs to be more distributed and that the structure and human resource systems will need to become more flexible. Without this flexibility, providing the right capability for the dynamic needs of the marketplace will prove both difficult and expensive.

Designing these more diverse and dynamic organisations will require greater transparency. Having a network map and a focus on work will provide essential transparency, allowing more detailed, higher quality organisational designs.

How should organisations manage people?

Companies seldom have the luxury of starting with a clean sheet of paper when it comes to managing people. In most cases, they start any discussion about policy and systems from a traditional hierarchical position. They typically have established processes for assembling teams with appropriate skills when clear job descriptions are available. They use recruiting and termination, internal and external training, and various techniques for issues of style and behaviour. They also have a wide range of competent external providers to support them in a range of disciplines.

To be effective, when more dynamic approaches are required, these processes need to be adapted to ensure that capabilities match the variety of work that needs to be completed across the organisation. To highlight the range of issues, we will compare traditional hierarchical and project-based organisations with outsourced communities.

Traditional capability management and development

Most people still work in a hierarchical organisation, as part of a team formed by reporting lines. They work either with the people who work for the same boss, or as part of a group that works across hierarchical silos. The hierarchical leader provides direction as appropriate.

Companies typically have well-established human resource management systems and processes to manage people and support capability development in these environments. These departments use job descriptions as a framework for recruiting, capability development and performance management.[131] When the work is relatively predictable, a job description can usefully describe the position in the hierarchy, the competencies required, and the list of accountabilities for the role. The work is implicitly understood because it changes little from year to year. This permits the performance of the incumbent to be assessed against generic key performance indicators, and be rewarded accordingly.

In this structure, careers progress in a linear fashion through functions and development roles, each step involving increasing ambiguity. With each year and step, status and compensation grow.

The work of creating teams and developing people is usually split between line managers and the human resource function on the basis of time horizon and organisational level.

- Line managers (usually with an HR partner) tend to focus on the operational aspects of their team's performance. These will include individual development plans, individual and team performance management programs, identification of capability gaps, and the development of plans to close these gaps.

- Corporate HR tends to be concerned with more strategic and policy matters, such as the creation of an overarching policy framework for human resource issues. These will have a general impact and will include governance, industrial agreements and compensation systems. It includes oversight, with the CEO, of the careers of the people in the top leadership cadres.

Key human resource functions in these organisations include organisational design, capability assessment, internal transfer or external recruitment, and learning and development. These processes can be represented by a cycle.

Role descriptions in complex environments

The success or failure of the traditional approach depends on the clarity and contextual relevance of each job description. Taken together, these job descriptions should provide a comprehensive description of the accountabilities and capabilities of most organisations. Collectively, they form a traditional model of organisational work in a stable environment.

In order to maintain a reasonable level of order in a changing environment, each job description needs to be maintained. As a role changes, leaders need to provide higher order direction to ensure the quality, relevance and structure of the job description.

When the work is reasonably stable, or the management team is mature and skilled, this input is relatively straightforward. A role-based approach to capability development is likely to be highly successful.

However, when the work is not straightforward, job descriptions can break down, becoming a poor basis for capability development and management. This can happen in a number of ways:

- The content of the job description can be generic, or out of date, and not suited to the current needs of the environment.

- The organisational structures in which the job exists can change, making the role more (or less) demanding.

- Leaders may be unable to describe what they want in detail. Role titles can no longer be used as shorthand for specific capabilities. Static competency standards are rarely flexible enough, or granular enough, to describe leadership work and executive capability.

- Compensation systems that reward people for their position in the hierarchy, or for the scale of their operation, distort incentives. This can occur at the expense of larger, but less measurable, types of value creation.

- HR professionals may not be clear about the organisation's specific needs and resort to generic profiles in order to meet deadlines.

At this point, the very strength of robust traditional systems and processes works against the organisation because line leaders will try to adjust quickly to accelerating changes in the environment. This usually results in mismatches of capability—and frustration.

In addition to the communication and knowledge management problems, a personal dimension exists. When work is described as a role and tailored to fit an individual, it becomes inflexible. As the priorities of the business evolve, it is difficult to separate discussion about the role from an evaluation of the person in that role. Any realignment of the work becomes personal for the incumbent, who may or may not have the capability to change. Feedback can be provided and capability can be adjusted more easily if it is not seen as a challenge to the incumbent's career or compensation.

A dynamic approach

Many firms that operate in volatile environments respond by organising dynamically around projects and project teams. Comparing hierarchical and dynamic approaches to people management helps to identify issues that leaders must address if they are to have the capabilities that they need consistently.

Consultancy firms, investment banks, contracting companies and other project-oriented organisations match capability directly to the needs of particular projects. In these organisations, people are managed dynamically so that an appropriate capability is available for each evolving project. Careers and development activities are built around cohorts and projects.

In this approach, project leaders are required to create a workable project team with the available capability, rather than being required to design a perfect team and expecting it to be provided by somebody else. HR leaders juggle scarce resources across multiple projects. Team composition is the result of the project design and capability planning processes, rather than a fixed hierarchy. To the extent that there is an organisational design, it is dynamic.

The key elements of this approach include:

- **cohorts**—In project-oriented organisations, titles are important only in so far as they designate an individual's capacity to work at a particular level. A wide range of executives might have the title of director, project manager or team leader. However, within these general cohorts, each will have different skills and capabilities and will be allocated to different kinds of projects. A career for a consultant consists of work of increasing criticality, in a series of projects, rather than a series of roles.

- **dynamic allocation**—This approach allows firms to dynamically place people and allocate capabilities to specific client problems, without any loss of status for the individuals involved. The services of better performing consultants may be requested first and the results may progress faster. But anybody can be allocated to any client, as need dictates. Client leaders can make changes quickly because personal implications for team members are limited. Individuals can move around and build a portfolio of skills and experience that suits them.

- **flexible hiring**—These organisations can hire people externally for specific projects as required. This allows them to introduce 'outsiders' who have the relevant capability and diversity, without disrupting organisational norms and creating inequities. Being able to introduce alternative points of view, cost-effectively, can materially improve the quality of a plan. Traditional hierarchies have trouble with this because it causes people to question the fairness of the various employment contracts.

- **supporting human resource systems**—Once hierarchical roles are replaced by project teams, performance and compensation management processes must follow suit. Annual evaluations will have less relevance than quarterly or project-based reviews. Rewards need to reflect both individual performance and collaborative contributions.

- **project feedback**—Finally, this project-based approach has the advantage of providing a less personal basis for feedback. Telling people that they did not perform well on a particular piece of work can potentially be much more fact based and less threatening than telling them that they are not good at their role.

A community-based approach

Social platforms, and the internet more generally, have created the potential for new and materially different organisational forms. These are most obvious in the technology industry where organisations like Wikipedia, Mozilla and Linux have created enormous value and disrupted major industries with little formal hierarchy. This new range of options expands the discussion of strategy and structure.

Here, communities of people are recruited internally and externally to solve various problems and perform various types of work. Every component of labour can now be outsourced. The value of everybody in an organisation can be compared to a global market.

When people work more independently, they find themselves contributing to a variety of pieces of work, based on favours and requests, as well as formal instructions. Their contribution becomes a portfolio of personal deliverables, short-term assignments, contributions to others, and some 'core' tasks.

This kind of contribution can prove difficult to align with traditional human resource systems and processes. Leaders and HR professionals need to find ways to be clear about:

- how to frame the work that people are supposed to do, so that their performance can be properly assessed and rewarded

- what capabilities are required to do this work and the development approaches that will be available to close capability gaps

- how human resource systems and processes align to fairly and efficiently support different kinds of work in different parts of the organisation (compensation, promotion, learning and development, discipline, etc.).

The most effective approach will probably be a mix

Companies will probably need a mix of approaches to create the best solution for their context. When there is one set of rules for everybody, this is relatively straightforward. It is much harder to manage different approaches within the same organisation.

The challenge comes when people on different career tracks need to work together collaboratively, either because a company needs to import different kinds of talent, or people with different approaches need to collaborate.

Increased flexibility means different rules for different people. As arrangements become more transparent, people will want to pick and choose from the various options, making life difficult for managers. During moments of conflict, it is easy to make promises that cannot be kept.

This conflict can challenge executional consistency and human resource discipline, undermining fairness, productivity and efficiency. The HR team's role in balancing flexibility and fairness in individual remuneration and development programs becomes critical. Most importantly, it is critical to control cost. To make any model succeed, operational leaders must develop a shared language with HR partners in order to discuss capability and to match people to the work in a way that is both effective and sufficiently dynamic.

Leaders are likely to be disappointed if they assume that employees already understand what needs to be done and on what basis they are being rewarded. In addition to clarifying what needs to be done, leaders need to explain why this work is important and valuable for the individuals involved. In some ways, a leader needs to treat everybody in their team as a volunteer who has a range of project options within, and outside, the enterprise. The most talented people will have more options and be more visible. If a leader cannot provide meaningful work and fair conditions for these individuals, they will have the means and 'permission' to move, without career consequences.

Beyond recognition and reward, people on different tracks also bring different expectations about decision rights, information flows and speed of decision making. If these expectations are not called out and managed, they can lead to dysfunctional interactions. Case Study 15 provides an example of this phenomenon.

Case Study 15
Running a contracting business in a manufacturing organisation

A major construction materials conglomerate ran a portfolio of businesses. These were predominantly manufacturing plants of various kinds: cement plants, quarries, and depots producing concrete and asphalt. The organisation also ran a series of installation contractors for laying concrete and paving roads.

The profitability of most of the organisation depended on manufacturing businesses that needed consistent, efficient execution of fixed plant and equipment. Hierarchical structures and clear job descriptions allowed the organisation to run effectively.

These approaches did not work well for the contracting parts of the businesses, however. The work of a contracting business is different. Here, leaders needed to be able to make deals and move people around the country, chasing work in real time. A cultural tension was created in the hierarchy when a contractor ended up working for a manufacturing leader.

The profitability of the contracting businesses varied in ways that were predictable. Each time a new manufacturing leader took oversight of a contracting operation, they enforced manufacturing policies and procedures. Profitability fell. The contractors would get frustrated and complain. Eventually, the manufacturing leader would come to understand the difference between the two operating models.

The problem was not solved until the company codified the differences in approach between the two kinds of operations and a management framework for each was created.

Organisational structure as a source of competitive advantage

The idea that structure and systems are important drivers of competitive performance is not new. In the 1990s, there were similar discussions regarding processes, teams and various production systems like SAP. The new generation of tools is simply continuing that discussion at the leadership level.

Organisational form and supporting processes are difficult to change, or copy. They can provide an enduring competitive advantage.[132] Leaders have to decide how broad and diverse the organisation that they create and support needs to be. Bigger and broader groups are more powerful if they can be appropriately aligned. However, capability diversity can be hard and expensive to create and maintain. Variety and flexibility need to be balanced with consistency, operational discipline and fairness.

Network-centred leadership helps with these design choices by providing a detailed map of the work that needs to be done. Companies that better match their leadership approach and organisation to the work should outperform those whose structures are either too rigid or too flexible.

When the leaders of an enterprise have a well-developed understanding of capability, there is a firm foundation for successful management and development. By contrast, confusion about what is required, or the perception of a negative implication for careers, is likely to lead to capability gaps and frustration among executives.

How should leadership be selected?

Who should run these more complicated organisations? If organisations are undertaking different kinds of work, they are likely to need a broader range of leaders. We consider that a capable executive should have four attributes. They should:

1. display good character, reflective of the values and behaviours of the organisation

2. bring relevant skills and experience, according to the work that they need to do[133]

3. contribute in a way that fits into the context of the team and the broader organisation

4. demonstrate good judgement.

The first two attributes are usually a product of the individual's historical experience, education and social environment. The third is typically role specific. The fourth attribute, good judgement, usually encompasses elements of each of the three preceding capabilities.

This model allows leaders to compare an individual's capability with the specific work and culture of a particular team or organisation, and to develop a capability gap closure plan for the individual (Table 3). In a traditional hierarchy, a job description should provide the details of the work and the capability requirements. However, in dynamic environments, this may be complemented by other documentation from particular hubs such as project charters.

Table 3. Framework for closing an individual's capability gaps

	Specific work requirements	Individual's capabilities and potential	Gap closure plan
Character			
Skills and experience			
Context			
Judgement			

Character

Character describes the moral qualities and personal traits that constitute the nature of a person. To some extent, character can be described through a list of attributes. For example, there are a number of profiling tools, such as the Life Styles Inventory or Myers-Briggs Type Indicator, that categorise leaders based on a variety of characteristics.

Once an executive reaches mid-career, his or her character will have become relatively stable. The best one can do to manage character issues is to raise an individual's self-awareness of his or her behaviours.

As a consequence, character has to be one of the central questions when recruiting. Leaders who are not compatible with the values and target behaviours of an organisation are unlikely to be successful within that organisation. The ability and willingness to collaborate is a simple instance of this phenomenon.

Requisite skills and experience

Skills are properly understood as being building blocks for any executive. Many disciplines, such as accounting, engineering and project management, have well-established approaches, frameworks and rules that leaders need to know. They are taught to individuals by a wide range of institutions.

We can think of this kind of knowledge acquisition as being like shopping. An individual goes out to acquire and own knowledge that is relevant to his or her career.

When leaders change their environment, there are likely to be gaps between an individual's prior skills and experience and the needs of the new work and environment. These gaps are most obvious when senior leaders are recruited externally. When work changes, leaders typically need to add relevant skills and experience to close specific gaps. A good example of this problem is when a move is made by functional or technical specialists to general management. In either case, the leader needs to 'go shopping'.

Shared context

Context has been described previously in Chapter 10. If people understand their context, they can more easily apply their skills in valuable ways and more fully contribute to teams and the broader organisation.

Context is learned in a different way to skills. Contextual learning typically takes place through a process of observation, application, reflection and modelling. It is a deeply social process whereby the learner and the environment are interdependent.[134]

Judgement

Judgement is the ability to make considered decisions and to come to sensible conclusions. If a leader has good judgement, they will be able to apply the right knowledge, at the right time, in order to deliver deserved results. It is the most important layer of capability, and the most difficult to develop.

Judgement in leaders is situational, practical and acquired through experience, as well as study.[135] It is usually developed by working in a specific role, under specific circumstances. And it is typically learned over time through a process of structured practice, feedback and study.[136]

Perhaps the single most important, and least understood, investment decision that leaders make today is the level of risk that they will tolerate when allowing emerging leaders to develop judgement.

How should leadership be developed?

There are common ways a line leader (and organisation) can support the development of a team: recruiting, providing feedback, skills development, structured practice and termination.

Focusing on work and drawing distinctions between character, skills, behaviours, context and judgement helps leaders use these tools to best effect.[137]

Recruiting

The model in Table 3 was developed through hundreds of executive search engagements. General job descriptions are only a starting point for strategy execution and major programs. In most cases, everybody in the room is intelligent, articulate and credentialed. Performance, capability and development need to be measured against the specific work of a team and its strategy, not a generic profile or theoretical model of capability.

Network maps and work patterns consistently deliver significantly better outcomes. They help to match candidates to roles and to identify precise skills gaps for ongoing development.

In addition to the description of what work needs to be done, companies also need to be clear about organisational structure and career progression. This helps candidates to understand how work will be conducted and also helps to ensure that they are a good fit for the particular environment.

Providing feedback

When companies are able to build explicit discussions about work and performance into their culture, they will have a major source of competitive advantage.

If a leader is aware of a gap or has built a strong team to cover it, they are likely to make the right decisions. If they are not aware of a gap, they are likely to fail. So the first challenge in any development program is helping leaders to know what they don't know. Until a leader is aware of a gap, they are unable to address it.

Network-centred leadership helps this process by providing a specific, impersonal framework for discussion. Rather than talking about individuals directly, it focuses on an individual's performance vis-à-vis a specific piece of work that is supported by a range of data points. Leaders who are unable, or unwilling, to address development issues directly may be able to have this more specific conversation.

Providing regular feedback during initial periods in a new role can also mitigate risk and give leaders the best possible chance to build the requisite capabilities that they need to be successful. This is harder than it seems because when leaders become more successful, they typically have fewer peers, or managers, to give them real feedback.

Organisations can assist this process by capturing the perspective of others above, below and alongside an executive. They can provide appropriate feedback as part of the organisational norm. At lower levels, it can be general, 360-degree feedback. At senior levels, it needs to be managed through specific pieces of work.

Ongoing teaching and learning

As the environment keeps changing, useful knowledge and habits quickly age. Leaders need to integrate teaching and learning into the fabric of their organisations, so leaders and teams can safely acquire capability in real time and longer term agility.[138] As importantly, leaders and teams need ways to 'unlearn' past practices and habits that may no longer be relevant.

There are now more ways than ever to close knowledge and skills gaps. Education is in a state of transition, with much of the educational content of the world available to everybody at quite low cost.

The next generation of leaders is well prepared for this kind of environment. Much of their education has been online and team based and many have spent numerous hours engaged in massively multiplayer online role-playing games. The idea of banding together in 'clans' to achieve a specific academic project or online quest has become second nature.

When they come to organisations, they bring deep expertise in collaboration, clan recruiting and formation, experimentation and adaption. More specifically, this generation of 'digital natives' is comfortable with using online platforms for collaboration and learning. Many see traditional management techniques and technologies as antiquated.

Companies like Shell, BP, GE, Dow Chemical Company and BHP Billiton are already making large investments to adjust corporate training and development to reflect these needs and opportunities. They are combining social platform online learning for skill acquisition with the use of corporate facilities. This helps to create a focus on collaboration and the sharing of experience and knowledge.

Online learning can to some extent deliver this training, but leaders will still need to develop the relevant materials and provide specific coaching to individuals, the team and the broader organisation. The challenge is to adapt training to the business context so that it can be readily adopted. Since the training is related to work that needs to be done, the content has to progress beyond the generic materials that most in-house campuses produce.

Hubs can be used as a basis for this ongoing training. Technically, social platforms can extend these conversations to larger and more distributed groups. The large amounts of contextual material that describe the real work of a team can be tightly integrated with relevant training materials. Content can be related to development at one moment, and deployed to the team for training in the next.

Social platforms provide new sources of data to support learning and development. Platforms can provide managers with in-depth metrics measuring the contribution that each team member has made to each piece of work over any period of time.

Learning how to use the new information from social platforms, in a fair and equitable way, will be an increasing challenge. The technology introduces a range of issues. It also has the potential to address the many issues of bias inherent in today's review processes. These changes have already occurred in industries in which measurement of individual performance is most critical, such as professional sports.[139]

Case Study 16 provides an example of how we used an online hub to facilitate a new CEO appointment.

Case Study 16
Minimising international transfer risk to accelerate CEO effectiveness

Our client, a major contracting firm, engaged us to find and orient a new CEO. The successful candidate in the global search was an international executive who had never worked in Australia.

The chairman was concerned about the transition risk associated with moving the person to a new company in a new country. He asked us to advise on how best to get the new appointee up to speed.

We created an online hub to support the transition, which involved starting a conversation between the CEO and the company about various elements of the move. Folios ranged from the mechanics of living in a new and foreign city, to the state of the enterprise, to the right way to approach the CEO's first 100 days. This allowed the incoming CEO to learn about the new environment before starting.

More importantly, we set up feedback mechanisms between the CEO and chairman to ensure that each became comfortable providing feedback to the other. We also provided feedback from our perspective.

The combination of these initiatives substantially reduced the risk for the chairman, the new CEO and the organisation. What really mattered was a shared understanding of the critical work and a basis for honest conversation between the new leader and the chair.

Deliberate practice

Being explicit about work provides leaders with opportunities to practise in a more structured environment. It allows them to learn using their real business problems, to struggle with their language and approach in a safe environment, and to benefit from real-time feedback and interventions. Gaps in skills and knowledge can be identified and addressed as part of these exercises. Or they can be dealt with via support from peers or traditional development.

In order to do this, organisations need to provide good measurement and context so that the practices can be structured and feedback can be fact based. Traditionally, progress and outcomes are measured through traditional reporting. However, these can often be too slow. Organisations cannot afford to wait months and years to see if a new appointment will work out. Measures of engagement and participation, and a range of other early indicators of success, are required.

Fortunately, web 2.0's 'organisational campuses' can close these gaps. One of the most significant benefits of using social platforms is that they gather and sensibly present a variety of data streams to assess performance and support development. Five kinds of measures are worth considering:

1. participation (essentially page views)

2. engagement (specific contributions to pieces of work such as posts to a forum)

3. capability (the quality of those contributions)

4. progress (completed units of work)

5. outcomes (business results).

These measures should be seen as a progression. The first three measures are faster, but less precise, than the latter two traditional measures. They provide a foundation for discussion, well before traditional measures are available. If applied with skill to a cohort, they can predict the success of leaders and strategies with reasonable accuracy, and much faster than conventional approaches.

At the organisational level, deliberate practice aids the development of leadership pipelines to underpin talent management. As firms have become larger, and functions more specialised, the number of general management roles in many organisations has steadily decreased. This means that leaders, while technically very capable, come to positions of general management with limited practice at integrating different skills into a coherent strategy.

If leadership pipelines are constructed around the work of critical roles at different levels of an organisation, and cohorts are moved through these positions, organisations can develop a portfolio of leadership options for more senior roles. This approach can substantially reduce succession risk.

Reallocation and termination

Reallocating or terminating employees who no longer fit with the direction of an organisation are some of the hardest challenges that a leader faces. The implications are profound for those involved and many leaders will avoid these decisions until it is too late. While this is an understandable reaction, leaders who can work through these challenges and make the necessary adjustments will have a competitive advantage over those who cannot.

Case Study 17 provides an example of how one leader went about clarifying values and work as a basis for building an effective team.

Case Study 17
Clarifying values to build a capable team

One of our clients was a newly appointed CEO who had been charged by the board with transforming the company's results. He wanted to know whether his team was up to the task.

We interviewed each of the senior leaders and discovered a toxic work environment. Individuals were focused on taking credit for shared work and blaming others for mistakes. As one leader put it, 'Around here, the game is more like *Survivor* than football'.

The CEO was a person of integrity who clarified expected behaviours and provided feedback to his team. Everybody was given opportunities to express their views and modify their behaviours. He did not attempt to address the many social issues that were in play directly.

Instead, he asked us to help clarify the work that needed to be done to deliver his vision. We then helped to identify how the gaps could be closed between the capabilities of the group and the work that needed to be done. Over time, gaps between work and capability, and between current and acceptable behaviours, became clear.

We helped to engage two executive search firms and a number of new managers were recruited. We then oriented the new leaders and adjusted the team to accommodate the new hires. This process took about 18 months, but it materially addressed the team's alignment and capability issues. The new team had both better capabilities and behaviours that were consistent with the new culture.

Chapter 13
Delivering results in a dynamic environment

'We're not that much smarter than we used to be, even though
we have much more information—and that means the real skill
now is learning how to pick out the useful information
[the signal] from all this noise.
Distinguishing the signal from the noise requires both
scientific knowledge and self-knowledge.' [140]
~ Nate Silver ~

The previous three chapters have started with a blank sheet of
paper and defined the organisation as a network of hubs. We
have looked at the design of the work that occurs at each hub
and how the relevant teams are developed so that they have the
skills and context to be effective. We now take the perspective
of the leader of a hub and discuss how to deliver results in a
dynamic environment.

How can leaders deliver results and navigate a rapidly evolving
environment to achieve longer term goals? Pilots have learned
to deal with this kind of challenge. The issues associated with
dynamic environments and cognitive overload have been a critical
focus of the airline industry since its earliest days.

When jets were invented, the challenge of flying a jet engine
plane was beyond the capabilities of any single person. Pilots could
not observe the environment and intuitively process all the inputs

required to guide the plane. A new control system was developed called 'fly by wire'.[141] This new approach moved the model of how to fly a plane from the pilot's head to the dashboard. The role and the work of the pilot were separated from the autopilot. Gauges aligned to key inputs and outputs were organised around the model so that information could be properly filtered to support the pilot's work.

This explicit model gave pilots more time to observe the environment and process the numerous complex information streams associated with jet engine planes without becoming overloaded. The pilot communicated adjustments to the model and then changes were communicated 'by wire' to various subsystems across the plane as required.

This idea is relevant to any leader who is working in a dynamic environment. Modern information systems and social platforms can model any kind of work environment. Effective filters and delegation can provide more time for observation, situational awareness and adaption. Network maps play the role of the autopilot, helping leaders make the transition to a more complex and connected global environment.[142]

The key parts of any change

Let's assume that a leader starts the year with a clear plan and a capable and aligned team. The plan provides:

- **a clear description of the external forces that shape the team or organisation** (e.g. market, economic, political, social and regulatory forces) and the assumptions that are being made about each force. A common error in many plans is that they are simply projections of the past, without consideration of dynamic forces, or of emerging threats.

- **a clear statement of non-negotiables**. When the environment changes, leaders need to be clear about what really matters. For example, there may be specific financial restrictions, such as debt covenants that trigger default when breached. Equally, remaining committed to the broader mission of the organisation may be the prime objective. Johnson & Johnson famously used their credo to guide them through a number of crises.

- **a few key measures and goals that describe success.** The military uses the concept of the 'main effort'. That is, if you were cut off from everything, where should you apply your main effort? It is fairly easy to clarify this point by counting the number of measures used on corporate scorecards. If the company has a large number of measures, it is unlikely that leaders have clarity about which ones really matter.

- **an appropriate range of scenarios for development.** Planning is like any investment. Teams don't have unlimited capacity to consider options.

- **key strategic choices and methods.** These may be choices around investments, target markets, methods of operation, or people management.

As the year progresses, the team will build on the initial plan. They will refine methods, train people, trial new products and services, and learn. They will also accumulate a knowledge base of documents, spreadsheets and presentations. Collectively, this knowledge forms the model of the team's or organisation's work.

At some point, a change in the environment will occur. While each situation and adjustment is unique, common behaviour patterns forecast how individuals, or teams, will react. Behavioural research shows that an individual or a team will go through predictable stages in coping with change (Figure 41).[143]

Figure 41. The behavioural stages of a strategic transition

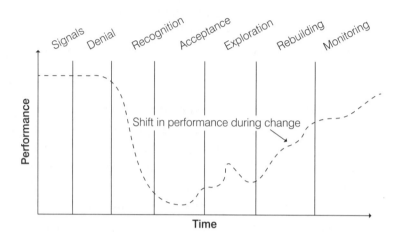

The shift in performance during changes consists of the following stages:

- **Observing signals**—The environment is changing. There are signals in the day-to-day 'noise' but they have not yet been identified by the leader, or the team, as being critical.

- **Denial**—The signals should have been identified, but the leader is unable to admit that a change has occurred. When those around the leader try to raise the issue, they are ignored.

- **Recognition**—The new reality is recognised, either because the leader is open and observant, or because it becomes public and/or unavoidable. Performance falls because of the changing environment and also because the targets change to reflect the new environment. Leaders may respond negatively at this point, with anger or blame.

- **Acceptance**—The leader and team accept the new environment and start to clarify what is occurring. Getting to this point may require changes in the composition of the leadership or the team.

- **Exploration**—New ways forward are explored. This may be new communication approaches, new products, new services or new financial arrangements.

- **Rebuilding**—A new approach has emerged and people are moving to align to the new direction.

- **Monitoring**—The new direction is in place and the appropriate targets are agreed.

Network-centred leadership assists with each stage of the change process.

Using an executive dashboard to observe signals

While every context is different, every good leader should have a dashboard of some kind. To create alignment, good dashboards will include risk frameworks, cascading goals, performance management targets, work plans and general reporting. The dashboard will help to manage information flows, monitor the environment for changes in context, monitor performance, and monitor for gaps in requisite capabilities. We will now look at each of these elements in turn.

Manage information flows

In the past, information was paper based, rare and valuable. Leaders could usually process most of what was available. That is now impossible because data continuously streams in electronically from a wide range of internal and external sources. The challenge is to find how best to filter all the available data and make sense of it.[144]

The solution to information overload is to filter sources of information based on the context, which is identified in each team's work model. Leaders should identify and watch the environment, the performance, the work, the capability of the team and the context of the hub.

The finite analytical capability of leaders, no matter how capable they are, is now only one critical resource for any team or organisation.

Monitor the environment for changes in context

Ideally, a leader will be aware of the relevant internal and external trends that are likely to affect a team. They can then identify what is the most relevant information by referring to their model.

There are many sources of valuable information now available. It is both easy and relatively cheap to assemble a precise set of information streams from Twitter, RSS feeds, internal systems and other channels onto a preferred device. This creates a real-time dashboard of the external environment. Potential inputs include:

- economic and geopolitical information on countries, markets, leaders and national statistics

- information about key customers, markets or industries

- traditional measures of performance from internal systems

- information on key competitors, or competitive technologies.

These information feeds can be assembled into any kind of social platform so that collectively they form a real-time dashboard for the team.

Meanwhile, the number of stakeholders is increasing. The use of social platforms gives power to the voices of dissenting minorities, which goes well beyond the historical ability of dissenters to influence executive decisions. Understanding this, and sorting out the valid from the mischievous, can be a significant drain on executive resources.

One of our clients, operating in several developed and emerging markets in a range of natural resource–based activities, created its own clearing house for contextual information. The strategic network map was overlaid on countries, projects and operations. An initial assessment was made of the associated political, country, market and technology risks for each. Trigger points were identified that enabled the business stream and corporate leadership to know when a venture could move from the infeasible to the highly desirable and vice versa. All project, operations and country leaders, together with the corporate marketing team, fed information on a daily basis to the clearing house. The CEO's view was that this information system was his organisation's greatest competitive advantage.

Monitor performance to confirm the quality of the plan

The bulk of performance reporting comes through a company's financial system and the associated review meetings. These reports and meetings are not free of bias and context.

One company (which is not a client) used a connected set of dashboards to manage a major enterprise. They then started to make both compensation and bonus decisions for the whole organisation from head office without an appreciation of the appropriate context. The results were neither fair nor effective.

A network map and driver tree can help to report financial performance in proper context (see Figure 28 in Chapter 9 for an example of a driver tree being used as a performance framework). More advanced companies run an independent, real-time model linking work to outcomes.

Driver trees provide a way to aggregate the financial impact of all the various work streams across an organisation. All too often, an organisation's strategic plan is devised by one group of leaders, while the operational plan is established by another group, leaving the issues of a changing environment unaddressed because they are 'out of scope' for both groups of leaders.

Meetings can be structured so that results are reviewed and discussed in context. Governance and reporting can clearly specify the relationship between the economic performance, the progress of the work and changes in the environment.

Monitor for gaps in requisite capabilities

Because leadership is context specific, individual differences between leaders, and the work that each is doing, should be monitored. If there are gaps, leadership risk will increase.

Signs of leadership risk include poorly communicated strategy, unclear accountabilities, silos and culture blocks, inadequate capability development, uncommitted leadership, unapproved strategy and incorrect skills or capabilities.

A simple matrix can be used to assess the level of leadership risk in a role, team or organisation (Figure 42). This is done by considering two dimensions:

1. **the clarity of the work needed to execute the strategy**. This addresses a leader's clarity around the work required, the alignment with his or her manager, the tasking of his or her team, and the agreements with key interfaces.

2. **a leader's 'fit' to the work of the role**. Can an incumbent bring and contribute the capabilities that the role requires today? Does he or she have the skills, experience and judgement to make the critical decisions? Can he or she contribute in this organisation, given its unique culture and approach?

Role clarity and a leader's capability are assessed on an individual basis. The review can be integrated with each organisation's human resource systems to allow performance management and development. It can also be used to assess leaders and close capability gaps.

By exercising judgement, the sum of the gaps can be aggregated to provide a perspective on the overall level of leadership risk in a team or organisation. This assessment has limits, however. It can only frame the probability that a business, strategy or initiative will fail because of inadequate or misaligned leadership. And it can only lead to informed discussion. Any more precise a claim is probably false precision. This is *not* an assessment of the overall capability of an executive, or of the overall level of risk in a business.

Figure 42. Assessment framework for leadership risk

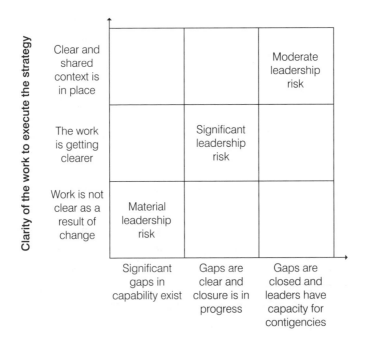

Case Study 18 describes how Waypoint uses information from its social platform to manage performance.

Case Study 18
Using a social platform to improve delivery

Over the past five years, we have had a development team consisting of a client in one city, a solution provider in another and a team of developers in India, using a Leadership Effectiveness and Elevation Platform (LEEP) program hub to support an agile development project. The hub provides ongoing training on the development method, technical design documents and project management records. Folios have been added and updated in an iterative manner to reflect changing requirements and lessons learned. The whole team has the most up-to-date project information 24/7.

As with any platform, it has been through a number of adjustments and redefinitions as various lessons about consulting, adult education and software development have been learned. Feedback from the social platform provides real-time feedback that has improved our performance, as shown in the following two examples.

1. **Activity measures provide an indication of engagement and learning**. This helps us to manage productivity across different companies and time zones. Figure 43 shows activity by the community. The dots represent changes to the technical program manager. The first project manager was a success. Activity spiked after his appointment until he emigrated. The second appointment was not successful. In this case, we were able to see the problem and react quickly. The LEEP hub provided clear data that enabled us to discuss the issue with the project manager and recognise a lack of fit.

Figure 43. Total activity at a LEEP program hub

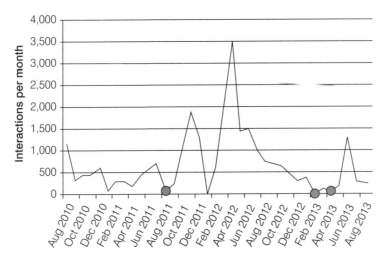

Change in technical program manager

2. **The LEEP program hub allows us to measure the creation of knowledge at a granular level**. Figure 44 shows the percentage of all activity that resulted in the addition of content to the hub. We can ensure that lessons learned are being captured and distributed to the team. We can be more confident that our investment is building a new digital capability.

Figure 44. Knowledge capture as a percentage of all activity at a LEEP program hub

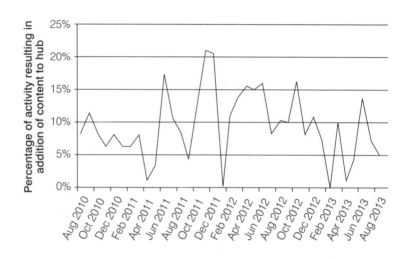

Recognising the need for change

As each year progresses, the environment will evolve. Typically, the degree of change will be within the scope of prepared scenarios and should be relatively easy to recognise. The more interesting challenge comes when the environment changes in ways that had not been considered, either because of a blind spot in the planning process or because of a 'black swan'[145] event that was outside the bounds of reasonable planning. Here, outstanding work can be wiped away by changes in the external environment, just as a rising market can hide a multitude of sins. (Discussions about 'performance-linked' executive compensation under these circumstances are rightly considered contentious.)

Each of the four kinds of leadership work described in this book requires character—wisdom, open-mindedness, integrity, fairness, humility and transparency.[146] However, these attributes are never more public and valuable than when the context changes materially.

Overcoming denial

Judging the difference between not overreacting to noise and being in denial is not easy. 'Everything is obvious in retrospect.'[147] Some leaders will not accept that reality has changed, despite a preponderance of evidence.[148] Others will react to every change, wasting energy.

The probability that a team (and leader) will be able to correctly recognise patterns earlier than competitors can be improved by creating better access to, and filtering of, information. It should be done by a team in a psychologically safe environment that encourages vigorous conversation. It helps to have a leader who is open-minded and whose actions are transparent.

Dealing with 'good luck' and reacting to 'bad news'

When change is favourable, the temptation is to relax and/or take credit for the positive trends. Humble leaders recognise their good fortune and manage it accordingly.

When change is not favourable, facing the brutal reality that goals will not be realised is difficult. Movies are full of scenes in which leaders go crazy at these critical moments. The range of defensive behaviours that may emerge include:

- **anger**—Anybody can make a mistake and apologise for it later. However, repeated, unsanctioned negative behaviours are particularly damaging for network-centred leadership, which should sit on a foundation of collaboration, psychological safety and integrity.

- **withdrawal**—Many leaders, suffering from cognitive overload, simply revert to embedded behaviours and finish up solving the wrong problem superbly well. Others will simply withdraw and stop collaborating.

- **blame**—People can avoid responsibility for their own behaviour, or situation, by blaming others. This is usually unhelpful and has a negative impact on psychological safety.

- **control**—When threatened, some leaders revert to traditional, hierarchical, top-down leadership behaviours and assume that they need to be 'in charge', and that this takes precedence over everything. In an emergency, they ensure that all decisions are centralised, essentially leading to upward delegation. Short-term survival mechanisms like this can have unintended consequences. Executives are often waiting to be told what they should do, even when the crisis is over.

Conversely, unfavourable times are the moments when leaders who maintain their operating disciplines can gain both kudos and competitive advantage.

Framing the magnitude of the change

Once a leader has recognised that a change has occurred, the second challenge is to assess its magnitude. Typically, this is done through a process of 'anchoring and adjusting'.[149] A leader or team will ask, 'How much of an impact can this change have?' This approach consistently underestimates the magnitude of the impact, leaving the leader to repeatedly go back to report bad news.

A wiser approach is to model the impact from first principles in order to build a range of possible outcomes and then to improve the quality of the estimate over time.

Managing the expectations of others

The denial process does not end when a leader accepts reality. They then need to discuss it with others, especially their hierarchical boss and potentially the board of directors. Each of these people will need to adapt in their own way.

In the traditional structure, these discussions used to be private. Those with power and position won any disagreement. In the internet age, they are becoming increasingly public. Both the manager and subordinate now face scrutiny of their behaviour.

Adapting to the new environment

Considerable judgement is clearly required to determine what constitutes an appropriate level of adaption to a particular change in the environment. At an organisational level, striking the right balance between control and flexibility is an ongoing challenge. If an organisation is too adaptable, it quickly becomes chaotic. If it is not adaptable enough, it soon loses its competitive position.[150]

Balance can be achieved through a combination of traditional management hierarchies and collaborative processes. These can be grouped into two types:

- amplification of effort through goals, initiatives, rewards and recognition (the plane's accelerator)

- dampening of effort through limiting decision rights, process rigour and hierarchical controls (the plane's brakes).

The right balance between these two tactics requires ongoing optimisation. Having too many goals and initiatives creates confusion, instability and chaos. Having too many controls can be stultifying. When change becomes continuous, trade-offs are typically managed through an initiative pipeline of some kind. The specific pipeline will depend on an organisation's critical resource. In mining companies, the capital approval process has an impact on the level and types of adaption being pursued. In the consumer packaged goods sector, where the attention of the sales organisation is a critical resource, the pipeline may be positions on the sales calendar. Or it may be the IT priorities that an organisation pursues.

Collaboration can help in times of adaption

Collaboration improves the probability of making a successful adjustment. It helps leaders and teams develop a range of options and scenarios. Returning to our plane analogy, this gives the pilot maximum flexibility to tailor the level and type of adjustments required. And it prepares the crew to execute a specific adjustment in real time.

As discussed previously, leaders who use a network-centred approach don't have to know the answer. They just have to be willing to ask the questions and work through the alternatives and consequences in a transparent manner. Capability diversity in a team is most valuable at this moment, as different frames of reference can assist when analysing the new environment.

As one client said:

> I couldn't help but think of a number of occasions where I might have done better by pausing before I took action to ask, 'What problem am I really trying to solve here?' Perhaps I've mellowed and grown wiser with age, but I no longer believe that I always know what to do. While it can be tough to admit you don't have all the answers, it's amazing how quickly the team of which you are a part aligns to develop a shared solution.

Modelling and open collaboration have the potential to test leaders at the best of times. At times of crisis, it is easy to revert to hierarchical control. Only if leaders keep their word at these moments will there be a psychologically safe environment in which trust can be maintained, and progress made.

Executing adjustments

When a leader (or a pilot) wants to make an adjustment, they should process information in four ways:[151]

1. They should observe a variation in the environment that may affect delivery (a signal as opposed to a lot of noise). Good leaders are continually interacting directly with the commercial and political environment. They are filtering what they see and hear with reference to their mental models, always looking for anomalies.

2. When a signal is inconsistent with their model, they first need to decide if it is consistent, or inconsistent, with the overall context. That is, they have to decide if the key assumptions on which the team or organisation is operating have changed. If they have, it suggests a need to redefine the current model and context.

3. If the context remains valid, the next question is, 'Does the signal change the base plan of the team or any of the options that the team is preparing?' If so, this new information can be used to redesign various plans, as appropriate.

4. Finally, a new signal may highlight where people have failed to properly execute agreed plans or options. In these cases, more development of the team or individuals may be required.

This approach to executing adjustments represents network-centred leadership's four-step approach applied in a recursive manner.[152]

Case Study 19 illustrates how network-centred leadership, rigorously applied, can deliver extraordinary results, despite profound market disruption.[153]

Case Study 19
Sustaining a transformation despite profound market disruption

We worked for over a decade with the CEO of a global resources company with operations in 178 countries. We started when he had just been appointed and the company was clawing its way out of a serious revenue and profitability problem that had been created, in part, by the bottoming out of a global commodity cycle.

The CEO had a very clear idea of why the company's performance had deteriorated and what needed to be done operationally and strategically to solve the problem. More broadly, the CEO's goal was to create a company that was protected from the ups and downs of the commodity markets. Achieving this involved transforming the company from a centrally run commodity business to a company consisting of multiple business portfolios, each with different kinds of competitive advantage.

We worked initially with the CEO and then a new team to identify the work that was required to deliver the vision. We helped to map both the tactical operational work and the broader strategic vision, then to put in place and elevate the evolving executive team.

The delivery of this vision involved the creation of separate business portfolios, each serving different customers with different value chains in each of their geographic markets. This introduced a variety of new competitive models and, with them, an increased level of variation across the organisation. In addition to the traditional 'low cost to serve' and operational excellence imperatives, the company needed to respond to technology-driven businesses as well as businesses that focused on customer and marketing intimacy.

The global financial crisis of 2007–2008 struck as the company was executing a major acquisition and a significant joint venture partnership, and making several material divestments. The buyer of a major part of the business withdrew, leaving an $8 billion cash gap. The markets that the potential target served began to collapse, as did the markets served by our client. Our client's share price plummeted. Short-term cash preservation became a critical, and dominant, imperative.

Despite this, the CEO was able to maintain the momentum of the transformation and deliver on his vision. The front-end rigour—clarifying and communicating the work that had to be done—and the various layers of capability development allowed his team to adjust without compromising its long-term objectives.

In the aftermath of the global financial crisis, the company found itself positioned to capture the benefits of faster growing specialist markets. While it had adjusted its implementation by stretching the timeframe, it had not lost sight of what it had to do to deliver on the vision.

Conclusion

'In times of profound change, the learners inherit the earth,
while the learned find themselves beautifully equipped to deal
with a world that no longer exists.'
- Eric Hoffer -

The world has become more complex and competitive over the past two decades. Regulatory and technical barriers to trade have fallen and markets have become increasingly global, intense and dynamic. In part, these changes are due to rapid advances in information technology. Social platforms are simply the latest step in this process, exposing knowledge workers to the same sort of competition that process workers have faced for some time.

Leaders need a new leadership approach to be successful in this environment. At the moment, too much is being expected from too few at the top of hierarchies. These individuals simply cannot process all the relevant information and make the necessary decisions in time.

Reframing the organisation as a network provides a better way to distribute leadership and manage work, capability, information flows and decision rights. Networks provide a mix of structure and flexibility that is superior to alternatives. They are a better way to organise people to deliver valuable knowledge work in complex environments. Networks also help to create and manage digital capabilities.

Network-centred leadership provides a structured way to apply this new approach. It is designed to work under the pressure and stress that dynamic environments often create. Practising this approach with your team members regularly will prepare both you and them for that moment when significant change occurs.

The key is to regularly make assumptions and mental models explicit. Turning what are often implicit insights and assumptions into good strategies requires deep interpersonal engagement and debate between leaders and their teams. While this can be difficult, it gets easier with practice. Many may find it difficult, but when leaders do slow down and engage their reasoning to discuss these questions, they will invariably do better than when they are simply running on instinct.

Once the context and work are clear, leaders can use social platforms to facilitate enterprise collaboration and create significant economic value. The challenge is to use these platforms in ways that respect the critical context and individual differences between leaders and teams that have such a material impact on executive performance.

Benefits of network-centred leadership revisited

It is worth repeating the benefits of network-centred leadership discussed in Chapter 9. Leaders who effectively implement a network-centred leadership approach will experience the following gains:

- **Accelerated effectiveness** in recognising and responding to problems, and at a lower cost, will give organisations a competitive edge.

- **Clearer context, goals and team roles** will accelerate and improve the quality and rigour of discussions, analysis, plans and solutions.

- **Better agility, innovation and growth** will arise from a common framework and language that helps everybody contribute appropriately to finding new solutions and closing specific skills gaps.

- **Long-term momentum** will develop, enabling leaders to apply their best thinking during periods of turbulence to protect performance, reduce risks and cultivate consistent behaviours that build trust throughout the change process.

A final comment

The era of the rigid, hierarchical business leader in a Napoleonic mould has long passed. In today's complex environments, leaders need to be able to adapt to different situations. An autocratic style may sometimes be required, but it is no longer a sure-fire way to win wars—the terrain has become far more complicated. Equally, collaboration is only necessary some of the time. People can't wait for a committee to discuss everything.

Leaders need to be able to shift between the different leadership modes—sometimes being like a conductor dictating to an orchestra in autocratic fashion, sometimes like a member of a string quartet working on a set of pieces, and sometimes like a leader of a jazz band in which everyone is left to play their own way and the outcome is only influenced, not controlled.

The framework described in this book helps with these new challenges. If applied regularly, it will consistently improve performance and help to mitigate career risk. The reality is that one in three leaders will fail in their new role, and one in three will perform below expectations. We hope that the time you have invested in examining network-centred leadership will help to ensure that you are in the third of leaders who excel.

Appendix
Further acknowledgements

The Waypoint Group would like to acknowledge the contribution that a wide range of individuals and organisations have made to our thinking, our firm and our online platform.

Our platform (both LEEP.net and much of the content in our library) is built on a collection of open-source and public domain technologies and we recognise the inherent copyright owned by others. Waypoint has taken legal advice to ensure that we properly use this material, and we have recorded the appropriate sources via links and other methods. However, it is possible that we have not properly reflected the contribution of some individuals or organisations. For this we apologise. If you believe that you, or additional authors, require acknowledgement, please contact Charles Carnegie on +61 2 9221 3000 so we can rectify the issue.

We recognise the following contributors.

The internet and World Wide Web
The internet owes much of its success to a collection of people who chose to give their technologies to the world, rather than to commercialise them. We would particularly like to acknowledge:

- Vint Cerf, and all who contributed to the internet protocols and institutions
- Sir Tim Berners-Lee and the founding members of the World Wide Web Consortium, who created the World Wide Web

- the individuals who pioneered and continue to promote open-source and/or Copyleft licences, which have provided the framework for both software and content to be shared with us. We regularly use the work of:
  - Richard Stallman and the Free Software Foundation
  - Creative Commons.

LAMP

LAMP, our operating environment, combines the work of several groups. We acknowledge everybody who contributed to its components, and we recognise any associated copyright. In particular, we recognise the developers of:

- Linux, especially Linus Torvalds
- the GNU General Public License
- Apache
- MySQL
- PHP.

Moodle

Moodle (https://moodle.org), our core application, is the work of Martin Dougiamas and the Moodle community. His personal support and encouragement was key to our selection of Moodle for our development. We recognise his trademark, and the copyright of all who have contributed to Moodle. We also recognise:

- Julian 'Moodleman' Ridden (http://moodleman.moodle. com.au/about-moodleman) for the Sky High theme
- the Nuvola blue icon set, which addressed a key issue at a critical time.

Beyond the platform, our thoughts on learning and teaching have been deeply influenced by Martin Dougiamas and the Moodle community at both the systemic and pedagogical level.

Content

The range of content that is made available under Creative Commons and other licences is astounding. We would particularly like to thank the following communities:

- Wikipedia (www.wikipedia.org)
- Creative Commons (https://creativecommons.org)
- Connexions (http://cnx.org)
- TED (www.ted.com).

On specific techniques

There have been many contributions to our approach. We are particularly grateful to:

- Hugh Morrow for introducing us to Moodle
- Amy Edmondson for introducing us to complex adaptive systems
- the folks at 37signals for introducing us to Christopher Alexander through their blog
- Mat Hunter for various military leadership concepts, including the OODA loop
- Andrew McDonald and Marcus McAuliffe for insights on driver tree models
- Dan Pontefract for assisting our thinking on online collaboration
- the outstanding professors at the University of Melbourne, the University of New South Wales, Harvard University and Stanford University, who provided our management and technical foundations.

Closer to home

We would also like to express our appreciation to:

- Scott McDougall, the contemporary artist who has allowed us to use his images on our website

- Hugh Morrow and all the team at Loaded Technologies
- Dick Sibbernsen, Anne Healy, Sue Durst and a number of other people at the Waypoint Group and its predecessor, McDonald Monahan Associates, who have contributed to the content of this book.

Abbreviations and acronyms

ADSL   asymmetric digital subscriber line
CEO   chief executive officer
GDP   gross domestic product
HR   human resources
IT   information technology
LEEP   Leadership Effectiveness and Elevation Platform
MBA   Master of Business Administration
OODA   observe, orient, decide and act
RSS   really simple syndication
S&P   Standard and Poor's

Glossary

The italicised words in the right-hand column appear as separate entries in the glossary.

Term	Meaning
adaption	the dynamic evolutionary *process* by which a team or organisation responds to a new environment outside the bounds of previous planning.
alignment	the extent to which the people in an organisation are doing work that targets the real goals of the organisation using agreed *methods* and *processes*.
altitude	the level of abstraction, breadth and/or complexity of a conversation.
approach	the way a *leader* executes his or her work; how leaders create and apply *mental models* to communicate with others. *Network-centred leadership* is one such approach.
'bring' factors	general behaviours and background that an individual brings to a role; e.g., skills (education and intellect), experience and *knowledge*.
business model	the standards and *patterns* that an organisation uses to work with its customers and create value. See Treacy and Wiersema (1997) for more detail.
'change the game'	opportunities to transform a company by radically changing the *business model* or transitioning to new markets; a paradigm shift.

Term	Meaning
'change the rules'	ways to exploit current industry 'givens'; e.g., changing the industry value chain or shifting market focus to adjacencies.
clarity	clearness or lucidity as to perception or understanding; freedom from indistinctness or ambiguity. Clarity implies a consistency of use across time and application.
coaching	the act of helping an individual to achieve certain goals, usually of a behavioural nature and frequently personally oriented.
cognitive overload	a condition where the demand of a situation or problem exceeds the mental processing capacity of a *leader*.
cohort	a group or band of people of a common generation as defined by years of experience, position or start date.
collaborative leadership	an *approach* to leadership that emphasises the ways teams can work together effectively in complex environments to create solutions in a highly flexible and interactive manner.
complex adaptive system	dynamic networks of interactions between agents of various kinds. They adapt to the changing environment.
complex organisation	an organisation that incorporates multiple structures. It is usually a matrix organisation complemented by project teams, cross-functional teams and other features.
compliance	the regulatory requirements and controls that need to be maintained to ensure that the management team meets its legal and statutory obligations.

Term	Meaning
context	the set of circumstances or facts that surround a particular team, *strategy* or *program* of work. It includes the current vision and goals of a team or organisation, language, *mental models*, specific historical agreements, goals and descriptions of the environment.
'contribute' factors	the behaviours and actions that a *leader* contributes to a particular team or organisation in order to be effective, typically as a reflection of a particular *context*.
corporate form	the shape or structure of an enterprise at the highest level.
critical role	a role in an organisation where decisions are taken that are material to the future of the organisation.
data	any unstructured bits and bytes. See also *knowledge*.
define	one of the four kinds of *network-centred leadership* work that involves analysing the environment and creating shared *context*.
deliver	one of the four kinds of *network-centred leadership* work that involves a controlled *approach* to produce desired outcomes, despite a dynamic environment.
design	one of the four kinds of *network-centred leadership* work that involves analysing alternatives and creating a clear *approach*.
develop	one of the four kinds of *network-centred leadership* work that involves creating a capable team with appropriate *leadership capability*.
double-loop learning	a *process* of learning where participants discuss both their *approach* and the key assumptions that underpin that approach. See also *single-loop learning*.

Term	Meaning
driver tree	a graphic way to represent different measures so that their underlying relationships are exposed for review.
enterprise collaboration	a way of working that combines *collaborative leadership* approaches with *social platforms*.
explicit	fully and clearly expressed, leaving nothing merely implied.
folio	an umbrella term for a piece of work that needs to be done; the folio may contain a variety of activities or tasks.
fractal	a rough *pattern* that can be split into parts, each of which is (at least approximately) a reduced-size copy of the whole, a property called self-similarity. A fractal pattern is built through a *recursive* process. The pattern need not exhibit exactly the same structure at all scales, but the same type of patterns must appear on all scales.
'get fit'	work to improve the current performance and commercial discipline of a team or organisation.
governance	a set of *processes*, customs, policies, laws and institutions affecting the way a corporation is directed, administered and controlled.
heuristics	see *mental model*.
hub	a place where a team can work on a specific *work stream*. It is also a node on a *network map*.
judgement	the ability to apply *knowledge* and act to *deliver* a desired outcome.
knowledge	information in *context*.
leader	a person in a business, organisation or enterprise who does *leadership work*.

Term	Meaning
leader elevation	the act of helping highly effective *leaders* navigate a challenge by clarifying their new environment, agreeing the priorities and *approach* with their manager, and then supporting progress against their critical priorities.
leadership capability	the requisite character, skills, experience and *judgement* needed to work effectively as a *leader* in a particular *context*.
leadership ladder	a visual representation of the *network-centred leadership* approach used to assess capability development in a team or organisation.
leadership risk	the probability that a business, *strategy* or initiative will fail as a result of inadequate or misaligned leadership.
leadership style	a *leader*'s distinctive or characteristic modes of action, which usually vary depending on the situation, and may be: • coercive (used in a crisis) • authoritative (often called 'visionary'— used to kick-start change) • affiliative (used to heal rifts in team behaviour) • democratic (used to build buy-in) • pacesetting (used to get quick results) • pedagogic (to help an individual improve performance).
leadership work	the work that a *leader* needs to do to positively answer the four questions of *network-centred leadership*.
level of work	the degree of ambiguity that needs to be addressed to successfully complete a piece of work. This falls naturally into five to seven levels in most companies. See Jaques (2006).

Term	Meaning
mental model	a conceptual representation of the past, present and future that can be evoked by language, and may include frameworks, *processes*, etc. (sometimes called 'heuristics').
mentoring	assistance provided by an experienced individual to a less experienced individual to deal with particular problems of a business or personal nature; particularly useful when an individual is confronted with new situations, such as a change in function, industry, geography, etc. It is effectively embedding a more senior person's experiences in a less experienced person to get them up to speed quickly.
method	a systematic procedure for achieving a result; usually a variety of alternative methods can be used to achieve a goal. Teams need to be clear on their chosen method to avoid miscommunication.
mission	see *vision*.
Moodle	an open-source online learning platform that underpins Waypoint's Leadership Effectiveness and Elevation Platform (LEEP.net). See https://moodle.org.
network-centred leadership	a four-step leadership *approach* that focuses on ways to *define*, *design*, *develop* and *deliver* work.
network map	a shared representation of various pieces of work that need to be completed to achieve the goals of the team or organisation. It helps to describe the *approach* that a *leader* and team *develop* to work together effectively.
owner intent	the long-term goals and intentions of the shareholders in total.

Term	Meaning
pattern	a way of representing information so that it can be reused in a new *context*.
process	a collection of related, structured activities or tasks that produce a specific service, or serve a particular goal, for a target group.
program	a collection of *projects* and *processes* that a team executes to *deliver* a particular set of outcomes.
project	a temporary activity, usually involving several parties, with a start date, goals, defined responsibilities, a budget, a plan, and a fixed end date.
purpose	see *vision*.
recursive	relating to a *process* or operation that can be repeated indefinitely in a self-similar or *fractal* way.
schema	see *mental model*.
self-similar	see *fractal*.
single-loop learning	a typical form of learning where people learn about a particular subject from an expert. See also *double-loop learning*.
social platforms	a collection of technologies and applications, characteristic of the second generation of the World Wide Web, that focus on collaboration, user-generated content and social networking.
strategic framework	a mental structure that groups similar activities in the aim of achieving a *strategy*. Our strategic framework involves three steps: • *get fit* and stay fit • *change the rules* • *change the game*.
strategy	a set of choices, applied over a period of time, designed to achieve a particular goal.

Term	Meaning
vision	a statement of a team or organisation's direction that may be expressed as a long-term goal or a future state. Often used interchangeably with 'mission', 'purpose' or 'strategic intent'.
waypoints	a set of coordinates that identify a point in space for the purpose of navigation. In a business context, waypoints may be strategic destinations, financial metrics or points in time, and can be used to help *define* 'invisible' execution plans for managing a company's direction.
work stream	a 'chunk' of work that needs to be completed by an organisation. It is represented as a *hub* on a *network map*.

Notes

Introduction

1   We have modified this quote to make it gender neutral.

2   Mankins and Steele (2005) analysed the causes of strategy failure. We attribute only 30% of the lost potential value of strategies to leadership failure, as the issue of inadequate or unavailable resources is often unclear.

3   The work in this case study was carried out by McDonald Monahan Associates.

Chapter 1

4   For a discussion on VUCA environments, see Wikipedia (www.wikipedia.org), 'Volatility, uncertainty, complexity and ambiguity' (accessed 18 April 2014). For a more detailed discussion of the issues, see Taleb (2012).

5   The increasing rate of 'creative destruction' is provided by Richard Foster. He is quoted in Antonio Regalado, 'Technology is wiping out companies faster than ever', *MIT Technology Review*, 10 September 2013, www.technologyreview.com/view/519226/technology-is-wiping-out-companies-faster-than-ever (accessed 18 April 2014).

6   Good examples of the relevant literature from the 1990s are Bartlett and Ghoshal (1998), who describe various kinds of matrix organisational structures in global companies, and Katzenbach and Smith (1993), who focus on the use of teams.

7   A discussion of the issues surrounding matrix structures is provided in Wolf and Egelhoff (2012).

8   The idea that complexity requires different leadership approaches is well described by Snowden and Boone (2007). They use the 'Cynefin' framework to describe complex environments in more detail and lay out how leaders might best progress in each environment. We have found their work to be an effective way to discuss complexity and leadership with our clients.

9   A number of significant and interesting case studies describing this phenomenon can be found in Tedlow (2010).

10   Cognitive overload is a symptom of a broad range of human errors including fear, guilt, greed or other psychological factors. It results in the misapplication of mental models, confusion and organisational misalignment. See Kets de Vries (2006).

11   Mental models (also called schemas or heuristics) can be of different kinds and at different psychological levels. For a general introduction to decision making, see Kahneman (2011).

12   For a summary of various psychological factors driving dysfunctional behaviours, see Kets de Vries (2006 and 2011).

13   The high failure rates of projects and programs have been verified in a number of studies. Kotter (1996) published research showing that only 30% of change programs were successful (i.e. were on time, on budget, and delivered the expected outcome). Turner and Crawford (1998) found that 88% of executives believed that the changes were right and their organisation was capable of achieving the changes, but only 33% achieved partial or complete success. Prosci (2005) studied 10,000 projects and reported that 29% were successful, 53% were challenged (i.e. were late, over budget, and/or delivered less than required) and 18% failed (i.e. were cancelled or delivered and never used). Fine, Hansen and Roggenhofer (2008) indicated that the success rate for change projects was still 30%. The Standish Group (2011) suggests that the success rate is 34%.

14   See note 2.

Chapter 2

15 The value of this kind of planning can be seen in Gawande (2009) or in John Cleese's presentation on the origin of creativity (2008).

16 For a description of bias in decision making, see Kahneman, Slovic and Tversky (1982), chapter 1, and the introduction to Gilovich, Griffin and Kahneman (2002). Alternatively, read the more accessible work by Kahneman (2011).

17 A discussion of the issues surrounding matrix structures is provided in Wolf and Egelhoff (2012).

18 In this book, the term 'social platform' refers to a second generation of social technologies and applications that are characteristic of web 2.0, featuring dynamic interaction and collaboration among users.

19 For a discussion on the opportunities provided by social platforms, see Wikipedia (www.wikipedia.org), 'Network-centric organization: Social technologies' (accessed 19 April 2014).

20 Social platforms had 65% penetration of corporations in 2009; see Chui and Bughin (2010).

21 There are a number of different quality methods, such as W. Edward Deming's plan–do–check–act approach.

22 The potential of a collaborative approach is well described in Argyris (1999) and Page (2008).

23 For a good general overview of the human fears and biases that can emerge during collaboration, see Kets de Vries (2011), chapter 6.

24 This can be referred to as the 'storming' stage in group development terms. See Kets de Vries (2011), page 112.

25 For a broader discussion of psychological safety, see Edmondson (1999).

26 This description is taken from Edmondson (2003), page 4.

27 See Wikipedia (www.wikipedia.org), 'Chatham House Rule' (accessed 20 April 2014).

28   For a discussion of the various kinds of 'facts' that are now available to support any position, see Weinberger (2012), chapter 2.

29   See interview with Laszlo Bock in Thomas Friedman, 'How to get a job at Google', *New York Times*, 22 February 2014, www.nytimes.com/2014/02/23/opinion/sunday/friedman-how-to-get-a-job-at-google.html?_r=0 (accessed 20 April 2014).

Chapter 3

30   Kotter (2012).

31   This outline of social platforms is taken from Chui and Bughin (2010).

32   In 2009, technology market research firm Gartner estimated that emerging technologies such as web 2.0 were two to five years from mainstream adoption—see Eric Auchard, 'Twitter backlash foretold', Reuters, 11 August 2009, http://blogs.reuters.com/commentaries/2009/08/11/twitter-backlash-foretold (accessed 20 April 2014). This is consistent with our own observations.

33   These platforms provide a range of other benefits; however, discussions on topics such as the advantages of software as a service are outside the scope of this book.

34   The need to consider online information and learning tools in a social context is well argued by Brown and Duguid (2002), chapter 5.

35   This claim about the value proposition supporting social platforms is provided by Cross and Gray (2013).

36   The limited benefits that companies have realised from social platforms are described by Chui, Manyika et al. (2012), page 45.

37   Contextual and social barriers to successful collaboration are discussed in Matson and Prusak (2010).

38   These social challenges are described in a variety of sources. See, for example, Chui, Manyika et al. (2012), page 121.

39   For more on the factors that support the use of groupware, see Orlikowski (1992).

40   For a discussion of advice-seeking behaviour and consequences for collaborative overload, see Cross and Gray (2013).

41   Cross and Gray (2013), pages 50–56.

42   For a broader discussion of sources of value and enabling factors, see Chui, Manyika et al. (2012).

43   A summary of overload in networked environments is provided by Cross and Gray (2013).

Chapter 4

44   See McAfee and Brynjolfsson (2008).

45   See Bradley, Dawson and Smit (2013), exhibit 8.

46   This summary draws heavily from the work of McAfee and Brynjolfsson (2008). A broader description of how these kinds of processes might occur is provided in Beinhocker (2007).

47   For a discussion on core capabilities, see Hamel and Prahalad (1994). They use the term 'core products' instead of core capabilities. We refer to capabilities because of the shift to a service-based economy since 1994. We are also influenced by Davis (1989), who adopts a similar approach by using 'subcomponent' as the key unit.

48   We recognise that Hamel and Prahalad (1994) specifically separated competencies and business units. However, because of the success of the authors' ideas, managing competencies is far more developed and business units are now more flexible than they were in 1994.

49   For a discussion of knowledge workers, see Johnson, Manyika and Yee (2005).

50   See Chui, Manyika et al. (2012).

51   See Lafley (2009).

52   See Andy Grove, 'What I've learned', *Esquire*, 1 May 2000, www.esquire.com/features/what-ive-learned/learned-andy-grove-0500 (accessed 20 April 2014).

53 These three business models are taken from Treacy and Wiersema (1997). We have drawn on text from their book to describe each of their models.

54 This paragraph paraphrases Treacy and Wiersema (1997).

55 These two paragraphs also paraphrase Treacy and Wiersema (1997).

56 See Johnson (2010) for a broader discussion of how networks impact innovation.

57 This paragraph paraphrases Treacy and Wiersema (1997).

Chapter 5

58 Network-centred leadership is supported by two models that help clarify our thinking and refine our approach. The first model is the self-similar cycle of creative destruction seen in complex adaptive systems. There are a number of different descriptions of the self-similar cycle. The ecological language of Marten (2001), chapter 4, seemed most compatible with our observations about ideas and markets. The second model is Bruce Tuckman's group development model (forming, storming, norming, performing). For a description of this model, see Wikipedia (www.wikipedia.org), 'Tuckman's stages of group development' (accessed 20 April 2014). We use Tuckman's model because it will be best known to our readers. We appreciate that his ideas are now 50 years old and have been developed and refined by others; see, for example, Edson (2010). There are also a number of valid alterations to this approach; see, for example, Kets de Vries (2011).

59 The financial services case study was conducted by McDonald Monahan Associates (Waypoint's predecessor). The diagrams provided are generic versions of the actual consulting work.

Chapter 6

60 For example, Andersen Consulting used and sold a 'waterfall' design methodology at this time, consisting of sequential

phases flowing downwards. See Wikipedia (www.wikipedia. org), 'Waterfall model' (accessed 21 April 2014).

61 For more on the various leadership and development methods that have powered the internet, such as encapsulation and object-oriented development, see Brooks (2010) and Raymond (2001).

62 The value of different lenses and relevant capability diversity is analysed by Page (2008), starting on page 13 and explored through the rest of the book.

63 A good discussion of the relative merits of different combinations of networks and matrixes can be found in Wolf and Egelhoff (2012).

64 For an overview of the research on issues associated with the qualification of business models, see Klang, Wallnöfer and Hacklin (2014).

65 In any communication, it is obviously important that the meaning of words, pictures, etc. is effectively communicated to the recipient. This is supported by a range of research from the field of semiotics and learning.

66 In general, the quality of a business model is inversely proportional to the amount of information that its description requires (Gleick, 2012).

67 Technically, this is 'syntactics'—relations among signs in formal structures.

68 Technically, this is 'semantics'—the relation between signs and the things to which they refer (their denotata, or meaning).

69 Technically, this is 'pragmatics'—the relation between signs and sign-using agents.

70 The case for repetition and consistency in communication is made by a variety of researchers, including Kotter (2012).

71 For example, Marten (2001) uses complexity science to describe changes in populations, which is relevant to all market populations.

72 For example, Haeckel (1999) uses complexity as a basis for leadership.

73 For example, Kahneman, Slovic and Tversky (1982) explore the subject of behavioural economics to explain failures in actual decision making under pressure.

74 For example, Senge (1994) describes the intersection of systems thinking and learning.

75 There is a spectrum of supporting research that describes the relationship between the formal hierarchy and informal social patterns or networks in an organisation. At one end, Kotter (2012) proposes two explicitly different systems. By contrast, Nadler's congruence model simply describes the two as the formal and informal parts of the organisation (Nadler and Tushman, 1997). Perhaps the most interesting discussion of the two approaches is Brown and Duguid (2002).

76 Because the network-centred leadership approach—where assumptions and mental models are clearly articulated and made explicit—is based on complex adaptive systems research, it is self-similar or fractal in nature. For a discussion of complex adaptive systems and fractals, see Wikipedia (www.wikipedia.org), 'Complex adaptive system' and 'Fractal' (accessed 21 April 2014).

77 Fractals may be exactly the same or nearly the same at different scales. The definition of fractal goes beyond self-similarity per se to exclude trivial self-similarity and include the idea of a detailed pattern repeating itself.

78 For more complete descriptions of leadership complexity, see Jaques' (2006) description of levels of work, or Jaques, Clement and Lessem (1994).

79 Because network-centred leadership is self-similar, a network is simply a hub at a lower level of altitude.

Chapter 7

80 While many practitioners may regard this definition of leadership as obvious, it is a new way of looking at a very complex topic. Subsequent notes provide supporting references for this approach.

81 These definitions of leadership reflect a range of sources, from reference works such Wikipedia and the *Oxford English Dictionary* to management theorists such as Peter Drucker.

82 There are many legitimate ways to describe leaders and leadership—for example, by focusing on traits, situational interaction, function, behaviour, power, vision and values, charisma and intelligence, among others. For more on these various descriptions of leaders and leadership, see Wikipedia (www.wikipedia.org), 'Leadership' (accessed 21 April 2014).

83 Johnson, Manyika and Yee (2005) estimate that approximately 41% of American employees are involved in judgement work of some kind.

84 This is consistent with the idea that leadership is an emergent activity that relates to the interactions between agents that lead to change. See Hazy, Goldstein and Lichtenstein (2007), chapter 8.

Chapter 8

85 Personal discussion.

86 Alexander (1964), pages 26–27.

87 See Argyris (1999) for a complete analysis of the issues preventing the adoption of collaboration and organisational learning.

88 For an example of this, see reporting on the culture at Google in Bock (2011).

89 Methods to develop business models through iteration are described in Ries (2011).

90 The idea of strategy as a portfolio of options is well covered in Luehrman (1998).

91 The need for a new collaborative approach is described in Edmondson (2008). She describes the desired approach as 'teaming'.

Chapter 9

92   This graph assumes that capability is normally distributed in a general population in such a way that approximately 16% of the population are more than a standard deviation from the mean.

93   For more detail on the value of repeatable models as a basis for strategic advantage, see Zook and Allen (2012).

94   For a discussion of stories as a basis for knowledge transfer, see Brown and Duguid (2002), chapter 4.

95   See Lewis (2003).

96   Sense and respond is described in detail by Haeckel (1999).

97   See Coleman (1998), chapter 5, for a theoretical discussion of the factors that influence the building of trust. Also see Coleman (1988) for a discussion of the interaction between social and human capital.

98   A good summary of the important impact of work design on engagement and fulfilment is in Csikszentmihalyi (2008), chapter 7.

Survey

99   There are a number of ways to describe capability maturity. Perhaps the most famous description is contained in the Capability Maturity Model Integration (CMMI) program that is administered and marketed by Carnegie Mellon University. While ours is deliberately different and less prescriptive, it can be used in the same way as CMMI. For more information on CMMI, see Wikipedia (www.wikipedia.org), 'Capability Maturity Model Integration' (accessed 21 April 2014).

Chapter 10

100   See Gleick (2012), chapter 1, for an excellent overview of the use of redundancy to mitigate the risk of miscommunication. Our point is that in traditional environments, overlapping habits and practices provide this kind of redundancy.

101 The impact of language and preference diversity on productivity has been well documented, from the biblical story of the tower of Babel, to Page (2008). Page describes the various kinds of diversity that exist and the various costs and benefits of each kind.

102 In complex adaptive systems theory, these well-designed 'chunks' are represented as agents. In software development, they are called objects.

103 A clear discussion of the relative strengths of hierarchies and networks runs through Brown and Duguid (2002).

104 An excellent description of networks as an organisational form is provided in Iannacci and Mitleton-Kelly (2005).

105 The importance of information flows and decision rights is covered in Neilson, Martin and Powers (2008).

106 This is typically referred to as the Dunbar number. See Dunbar (2010).

107 For a discussion of the relationship between network connectivity and stability, see Beinhocker (2007), chapter 7, or Carroll and Burton (2000).

108 For a broader discussion of governance issues at the board level, see McDonald, Richmond and Sibbernsen (2006).

109 The importance of meaning and belonging in a role is described in Kets de Vries (2006).

110 Because the network-centred leadership approach is based on complex adaptive systems research, it is self-similar or fractal in nature (see Chapter 6).

111 Again, for more complete descriptions of leadership complexity, see Jaques' (2006) description of levels of work, or Jaques, Clement and Lessem (1994).

112 These three generic strategies have emerged from our consulting and are consistent with the control system model.

Chapter 11

113 A parallel description of this kind of approach is covered in Valentine and Edmondson (2013), who provide a

summary of the relevant research literature. They use the term 'scaffold' instead of hub.

114 A summary of patterns that are common in growth and innovation work is provided on Waypoint's website (www. waypointgroup.com.au). For more on innovation, marketing and agile management techniques, see, for example, Christensen and Raynor (2003) and Martin (2009).

115 This process is sometimes called 'norming' in the context of team development. See Kets de Vries (2011), page 112.

116 The importance of framing is well described in Douglas (2007), and is more fully supported in Kahneman (2011), Kahneman, Slovic and Tversky (1982), and Gilovich, Griffin and Kahneman (2002).

117 This is an idea that is well developed by the Moodle community. See Moodle, 'Pedagogy', http://docs.moodle. org/26/en/Pedagogy (accessed 22 April 2014).

118 The challenges associated with creating social cohesion are covered by Dunbar (2010) and Coleman (1988).

119 Neilson, Martin and Powers (2008) discuss the importance of decision rights and information flows for successful strategy execution.

120 These are 'forms'. For a related discussion of the difference between pattern languages and form languages in architecture, see Salingaros (2013).

121 The difference between a simple process and a process applied with judgement is well covered in Hall and Johnson (2009).

122 See Weinberger (2012), chapter 5, for a discussion of the problem of unlimited diversity of opinion.

123 For more on the transferability of social capital in organisations, see Coleman (1988).

124 For architecture, see Alexander, Ishikawa and Silverstein (1977), and for software development, see Buschmann, Henney and Schmidt (2007).

125 This thinking is very much based on the work of Alexander (1964) and Alexander, Ishikawa and Silverstein (1977). See also Wikipedia (www.wikipedia.org), 'Pattern (architecture)' and 'Architectural pattern' (accessed 23 April 2014).

126 Finding designs that overcome conflicting objectives is explored in greater detail as 'design thinking'. For an introduction to this subject, see Martin (2007 and 2009).

127 These stages of knowledge development are described in Martin (2009).

128 Distilling information into patterns releases capacity and reduces confusion, but requires work. This is consistent with Gleick (2012), who treats information as entropy, i.e. the inability to do work. Working to distil information into patterns improves the value of the knowledge and reduces confusion.

129 See Hall and Johnson (2009) for a discussion of how services can balance consistency with customisation.

130 The value of reusable patterns is described in Zook and Allen (2012).

Chapter 12

131 There is much confusion in both the literature and in practice about how to describe the work of a role: 'job description', 'position description' and 'position specification' are all used interchangeably. This book uses 'job description' as the general term that a person might use to describe general tasks, or functions, and responsibilities of a position (i.e. the work).

132 The use of technology and organisational form to create competitive advantage is discussed in Johnson, Manyika and Yee (2005); a more technical description is provided in Galunic and Rodan (1998).

133 We use a broad definition of skills here, including intelligence (IQ), emotional quotient (EQ), specific relationships, technical skills and people skills.

134 A good description of contextual learning is in Edmondson (2012).

135 This simple sentence on the development of judgement is derived from our experience and a number of sources, notably Argyris (1999), and Kahneman, Slovic and Tversky (1982).

136 For a full description of deliberate practice, see Gladwell (2008).

137 A good summary of the different kinds of capability is in Smith (2003). We have paraphrased some of his work in this description of learning.

138 The case for ongoing integrated learning is made in Edmondson (2008).

139 For a discussion of the impact of better measurement on the sport of baseball, see Lewis (2003).

Chapter 13

140 These two sentences are separate quotes that we have combined. See NPR, '"Signal" and "noise": Prediction as art and science', 10 October 2012, www.npr. org/2012/10/10/162594751/signal-and-noise-prediction-as-art-and-science (accessed 11 May 2014), and Silver (2012), page 453.

141 Fly by wire is well described by Haeckel (1999), page 163.

142 The proposition that military ideas on complex global environments can apply to civilian organisations is well explored by Menotti (2004).

143 Adapted from the five stages of grief in Kübler-Ross (1969).

144 A good summary of the challenge of filtering all of the available information in the most valuable way is covered in Johnson (2012).

145 For a discussion of uncertainty and 'black swans', see Taleb (2012).

146 For a more detailed discussion of character in general, and these traits in particular, see Peterson and Seligman (2004).

147 This phrase is taken from the title of Watts (2011).

148 For various historical examples of denial, see Tedlow (2010).

149 For more on anchoring and adjusting, see Kahneman (2011); Gilovich, Griffin and Kahneman (2002); and Kahneman, Slovic and Tversky (1982).

150 Carroll and Burton (2000) show that the number of interfaces linking a network of hubs is a key determinant of adaptability and that the optimum level of interdependence is relatively low.

151 This is the 'OODA' loop (observe, orient, decide and act) recommended for pilots. See Haeckel (1999).

152 Viewed from the perspective of a leader operating in a role, network-centred leadership is consistent with the OODA loop described by Haeckel (1999).

153 The global financial crisis case study was conducted by McDonald Monahan Associates (Waypoint's predecessor).

References

Alexander, C. (1964). *Notes on the Synthesis of Form*. Cambridge, MA: Harvard University Press.

Alexander, C., Ishikawa, S., & Silverstein, M. (1977). *A Pattern Language: Towns, buildings, construction*. New York: Oxford University Press.

Argyris, C. (1999). *On Organizational Learning* (2nd edn). Cambridge, MA: Blackwell Business.

Bartlett, C. A., & Ghoshal, S. (1998). *Managing Across Borders: The transnational solution*. Boston: Harvard Business School Press.

Beinhocker, E. D. (2007). *The Origin of Wealth: Evolution, complexity, and the radical remaking of economics*. Boston: Harvard Business School Press.

Bock, L. (2011, September). 'Passion, not perks'. *Think Quarterly: The People Issue*. Google Think Insights. www. google.com/think/articles/passion-not-perks.html (accessed 17 April 2014).

Bradley, C., Dawson, A., & Smit, S. (2013, October). 'The strategic yardstick you can't afford to ignore'. *McKinsey Quarterly*. www.mckinsey.com/insights/strategy/the_strategic_yardstick_ you_cant_afford_to_ignore (accessed 20 April 2014).

Brooks, F. P. (2010). *The Design of Design: Essays from a computer scientist*. Reading, MA: Addison-Wesley Professional.

Brown, J. S., & Duguid, P. (2002). *The Social Life of Information*. Boston: Harvard Business School Press.

Buschmann, F., Henney, K., & Schmidt, D. C. (2007). *Pattern-Oriented Software Architecture: A pattern language for distributed computing*. Chichester, West Sussex: John Wiley & Sons.

Carroll, T., & Burton, R. (2000, December). 'Organization and complexity: Searching for the edge of chaos'. *Computational and Mathematical Organization Theory* 6 (4): 319–337.

Christensen, C. M., & Raynor, M. E. (2003). *The Innovator's Solution: Creating and sustaining successful growth.* Boston: Harvard Business School Press.

Chui, M., & Bughin, J. (2010, December). 'The rise of the networked enterprise: Web 2.0 finds its payday'. *McKinsey Quarterly.* www.mckinsey.com/insights/high_tech_telecoms_internet/the_rise_of_the_networked_enterprise_web_20_finds_its_payday (accessed 17 April 2014).

Chui, M., Manyika, J. M., et al. (2012, July). *The Social Economy: Unlocking value and productivity through social technologies.* McKinsey Global Institute, McKinsey & Company. www.mckinsey.com/insights/high_tech_telecoms_internet/the_social_economy (accessed 17 April 2014).

Cleese, J. (2008). 'The origin of creativity'. Speech to Creativity World Forum, Antwerp, Belgium, 19 November 2008. YouTube video. www.youtube.com/watch?v=zGt3-fxOvug (accessed 17 April 2014).

Coleman, J. S. (1988), 'Social capital in the creation of human capital'. *The American Journal of Sociology* 94: S95–S120 (Supplement: Organizations and Institutions: Sociological and Economic Approaches to the Analysis of Social Structure). http://onemvweb.com/sources/sources/social_capital.pdf (accessed 22 April 2014).

Coleman, J. S. (1998). *Foundations of Social Theory.* Cambridge, MA: Belknap Press of Harvard University Press.

Cross, R., & Gray, P. (2013, Fall). 'Where has the time gone? Addressing collaboration overload in a networked economy'. *California Management Review* 56 (1): 50–66.

Csikszentmihalyi, M. (2008). *Flow: The psychology of optimal experience.* New York: HarperCollins.

Davis, S. (1989). *Future Perfect.* New York: Basic Books.

Douglas, K. (2007, December). 'The subconscious mind: Your

unsung hero'. *New Scientist* 2632: 42–46.

Dunbar, R. (2010). *How Many Friends Does One Person Need? Dunbar's number and other evolutionary quirks.* Cambridge, MA: Harvard University Press.

Edmondson, A. C. (1999, June). 'Psychological safety and learning behavior in work teams'. *Administrative Science Quarterly* 44 (2): 350–383.

Edmondson, A. C. (2003). 'Psychological safety, trust, and learning in organizations: A group-level lens'. Paper (5 May 2003). http://citeseerx.ist.psu.edu/viewdoc/download?doi=10.1.1.195.4023&rep=rep1&type=pdf (accessed 17 April 2014).

Edmondson, A. C. (2008, July–August). 'The competitive imperative of learning'. *Harvard Business Review* 86 (7–8): 60–67.

Edmondson, A. C. (2012). *Teaming: How organizations learn, innovate, and compete in the knowledge economy.* Hoboken, NJ: Jossey-Bass.

Edson, M. C. (2010). 'Group development: A complex adaptive systems perspective'. *Proceedings of the 54th Meeting of the International Society for the System Sciences.* Waterloo, Canada. http://journals.isss.org/index.php/proceedings54th/article/viewFile/1435/490 (accessed 17 April 2014).

Fine, D., Hansen, M. A., & Roggenhofer, S. (2008, November). 'From lean to lasting: Making operational improvements stick'. *McKinsey Quarterly.* www.mckinsey.com/insights/operations/from_lean_to_lasting_making_operational_improvements_stick (accessed 17 April 2014).

Galunic, D. C., & Rodan, S. (1998, December). 'Resource recombinations in the firm: Knowledge structures and the potential for Schumpeterian innovation'. *Strategic Management Journal* 19 (12): 1193–1201.

Gawande, A. (2009). *The Checklist Manifesto: How to get things right.* New York: Picador.

Gilovich, T., Griffin, D. W., & Kahneman, D. (eds) (2002). *Heuristics and Biases: The psychology of intuitive judgment.* New

York: Cambridge University Press.

Gladwell, M. (2008). *Outliers: The story of success*. New York: Little, Brown and Company.

Gleick, J. (2012). *The Information: A history, a theory, a flood*. New York: Vintage.

Haeckel, S. H. (1999). *Adaptive Enterprise: Creating and leading sense-and-respond organisations*. Boston: Harvard Business School Press.

Hall, J. M., & Johnson, M. E. (2009, March). 'When should a process be art, not science?' *Harvard Business Review* 87 (3): 58–65.

Hamel, G., & Prahalad, C. K. (1994). *Competing for the Future*. Boston: Harvard Business School Press.

Hazy, J. K., Goldstein, J. A., & Lichtenstein, B. B. (eds) (2007). *Complex Systems Leadership Theory: New perspectives from complexity science on social and organizational effectiveness*. Mansfield, MA: ISCE Publishing.

Iannacci, F., & Mitleton-Kelly, E. (2005, May). 'Beyond markets and firms: The emergence of open source networks'. *First Monday* 10 (5). http://firstmonday.org/article/view/1237/1157 (accessed 17 April 2014).

Jaques, E. (2006). *Requisite Organization: A total system for managerial organization and managerial leadership for the 21st century*. Arlington, VA: Cason Hall.

Jaques, E., Clement, S., & Lessem, R. (1994). *Executive Leadership: A practical guide to managing complexity*. Hoboken, NJ: Wiley-Blackwell.

Johnson, B. C., Manyika, J. M., & Yee, L. A. (2005, November). 'The next revolution in interactions'. *McKinsey Quarterly*. www.mckinsey.com/insights/organization/the_next_revolution_in_interactions (accessed 17 April 2014).

Johnson, C. A. (2012). *The Information Diet: A case for conscious consumption*. Sebastopol, CA: O'Reilly Media.

Johnson, S. (2010). *Where Good Ideas Come From: The natural history of innovation*. New York: Penguin Group.

Kahneman, D. (2011). *Thinking, Fast and Slow.* New York: Farrar, Straus and Giroux.

Kahneman, D., Slovic, P., & Tversky, A. (eds) (1982). *Judgment under Uncertainty: Heuristics and biases.* Cambridge, UK: Cambridge University Press.

Katzenbach, J. R., & Smith, D. K. (1993). *The Wisdom of Teams: Creating the high-performance organization.* Boston: Harvard Business School Press.

Kets de Vries, M. (2006). *The Leader on the Couch: A clinical approach to changing people and organizations.* Hoboken, NJ: John Wiley & Sons.

Kets de Vries, M. (2011). *The Hedgehog Effect: The secrets of building high performance teams.* Hoboken, NJ: Jossey-Bass.

Klang, D., Wallnöfer, M., & Hacklin, F. (2014, January). 'The business model paradox: A systematic review and exploration of antecedents'. *International Journal of Management Reviews.* DOI: 10.1111/ijmr.12030.

Kotter, J. P. (1996). *Leading Change.* Boston: Harvard Business School Press.

Kotter, J. P. (2012, November). 'Accelerate! How the most innovative companies capitalize on today's rapid-fire strategic challenges—and still make their numbers'. *Harvard Business Review* 90 (11).

Kübler-Ross, E. (1969). *On Death and Dying.* New York: Simon & Schuster/Touchstone.

Lafley, A. G. (2009, May). 'What only the CEO can do'. *Harvard Business Review* 87 (5): 54–62.

Lewis, M. (2003). *Moneyball: The art of winning an unfair game.* New York: W. W. Norton & Company.

Luehrman, T. A. (1998, September). 'Strategy as a portfolio of real options'. *Harvard Business Review* 76 (9): 89–101.

Mankins, M. C., & Steele, R. (2005, July–August). 'Turning great strategy into great performance'. *Harvard Business Review* 83 (7–8): 64–73.

Marten, G. G. (2001). *Human Ecology: Basic concepts for sustainable development*. London: Earthscan Publications.

Martin, R. L. (2007, June). 'How successful leaders think'. *Harvard Business Review* 85 (6): 60–67.

Martin, R. L. (2009). *The Design of Business: Why design thinking is the next competitive advantage*. Boston: Harvard Business School Press.

Matson, E., & Prusak, L. (2010, September). 'Boosting the productivity of knowledge workers'. *McKinsey Quarterly*. www.mckinsey.com/insights/organization/boosting_the_productivity_of_knowledge_workers (accessed 17 April 2014).

McAfee, A., & Brynjolfsson, E. (2008, July–August). 'Investing in the IT that makes a competitive difference'. *Harvard Business Review* 86 (7).

McDonald, D., Richmond, M., & Sibbernsen, D. (2006). *Reprogramming the Board: A comprehensive approach to aligning a company's board of directors and management team*. Boston: Aspatore Books.

Menotti, M. J. (2004, August). 'The sense-and-respond enterprise: Why the U.S. Marine Corps should embrace the new paradigm'. *Operations Research and Management Science Today* 31 (4). www.orms-today.org/orms-8-04/enterprise.html (accessed 4 June 2014).

Nadler, D. A., & Tushman, M. L. (1997). *Competing by Design: The power of organizational architecture*. Oxford: Oxford University Press.

Neilson, G. L., Martin, K. L., & Powers, E. (2008, June). 'The secrets to successful strategy execution'. *Harvard Business Review* 86 (6): 60–71.

Orlikowski, W. J. (1992, May). 'Learning from notes: Organisational issues in groupware implementation'. Massachusetts Institute of Technology Sloan School Working Paper #3428-92. Center for Coordination Science Technical Report #134. Cambridge, MA: Sloan School of Management. http://ccs.mit.edu/papers/CCSWP134.html (accessed 17 April 2014).

Page, S. E. (2008). *The Difference: How the power of diversity creates better groups, firms, schools, and societies*. Princeton, NJ: Princeton University Press.

Peterson, C., & Seligman, M. E. (2004). *Character Strengths and Virtues: A handbook and classification*. Washington, DC: Oxford University Press.

Prosci. (2005). *Best Practices in Change Management*. Loveland, CO: Prosci.

Raymond, E. S. (2001). *The Cathedral and the Bazaar: Musings on Linux and open source by an accidental revolutionary*. Sebastopol, CA: O'Reilly Media.

Ries, E. (2011). *The Lean Startup: How today's entrepreneurs use continuous innovation to create radically successful businesses*. New York: Crown Business.

Salingaros, N. A. (2013). *Unified Architectural Theory: Form, language, complexity*. Portland: Sustasis Press, OR Vajra Books: Kathmandu, Nepal.

Senge, P. M. (1994). *The Fifth Discipline: The art and practice of the learning organization*. New York: Crown Business.

Silver, N. (2012). *The Signal and the Noise: Why most predictions fail—but some don't*. New York: Penguin Press.

Smith, M. K. (2003). 'Learning theory: Models, product and process'. In *The Encyclopedia of Informal Education*. http://infed.org/mobi/learning-theory-models-product-and-process (accessed 17 April 2014).

Snowden, D. J., & Boone, M. E. (2007, November). 'A leader's framework for decision making'. *Harvard Business Review* 85 (11): 68–76.

Standish Group. (2011). *CHAOS Report*. http://blog.standishgroup.com.

Taleb, N. N. (2012). *Antifragile: Things that gain from disorder*. New York: Random House.

Tedlow, R. S. (2010). *Denial: Why business leaders fail to look facts in the face—and what to do about it*. New York: Penguin Group.

Treacy, M., & Wiersema, F. (1997). *The Discipline of Market Leaders: Choose your customers, narrow your focus, dominate your market.* New York: Basic Books.

Turner, D., & Crawford, M. (1998). *Change Power: Capabilities that drive corporate renewal.* Warriewood, NSW: Business & Professional Publishing.

Valentine, M. A., & Edmondson, A. C. (2013). 'Team scaffolds: How minimal team structures enable role-based coordination'. Harvard Business School Working Paper 12-062. www.hbs.edu/faculty/Publication%20Files/12-062_80c30e9c-a309-47d9-86a7-06858c5ae804.pdf (accessed 17 April 2014).

Watts, D. J. (2011). *Everything Is Obvious: How common sense fails us.* New York: Random House.

Weinberger, D. (2012). *Too Big to Know: Rethinking knowledge now that the facts aren't the facts, experts are everywhere, and the smartest person in the room is the room.* New York: Basic Books.

Wolf, J., & Egelhoff, W. G. (2012). 'Network or matrix? How information-processing theory can help MNCs answer this question'. In A. Bøllingtoft, L. Donaldson, G. P. Huber, D. Håkonsson, & C. C. Snow (eds). *Collaborative Communities of Firms: Purpose, process, and design.* New York: Springer.

Zook, C., & Allen, J. (2012). *Repeatability: Building enduring businesses for a world of constant change.* Boston: Harvard Business Review Press.

Further reading

Adizes, I. (1989). *Corporate Lifecycles: Why organizations grow and die and what to do about it.* Paramus, NJ: Prentice Hall.

Baghai, M., Coley, S., & White, D. (1999). *The Alchemy of Growth: Practical insights for building the enduring enterprise.* London: Orion Business.

De Pree, M. (2004). *Leadership Is an Art.* New York: Doubleday.

Gill, B. (2013, June). 'Vision statement: E-mail: not dead, evolving'. *Harvard Business Review* 91 (6): 32–33.

Hagel, J., & Brown, J. S. (2005). *The Only Sustainable Edge: Why business strategy depends on productive friction and dynamic specialization.* Boston: Harvard Business School Press.

Mankins, M. C. (2004, September). 'Stop wasting valuable time'. *Harvard Business Review* 82 (9): 58–67.

Nonaka, I., & Takeuchi, H. (1995). *The Knowledge-Creating Company: How Japanese companies create the dynamics of innovation.* Oxford: Oxford University Press.

Rumelt, R. (2011). *Good Strategy, Bad Strategy: The difference and why it matters.* New York: Random House.

Schneider, M., & Somers, M. (2006). 'Organisations as complex adaptive systems: Implications of complex theory for leadership research'. *The Leadership Quarterly* 17: 351–365.

Index